Y0-BEB-097

J. M. HODGES LIBRARY
WHARTON COUNTY JUNIOR COLLEGE
WHARTON, TEXAS

A liberal answer to the conservative challenge

Eugene J. McCarthy

21483

FREDERICK A. PRAEGER, *Publishers*
New York • Washington • London

J. M. HODGES LIBRARY
WHARTON COUNTY JUNIOR COLLEGE
WHARTON, TEXAS

$3.95 Baker & Taylor (NDEA)

FREDERICK A. PRAEGER, *Publishers*
111 Fourth Avenue, New York 3, N.Y., U.S.A.
77–79 Charlotte Street, London W.1, England

Published in the United States of America in 1965
by Frederick A. Praeger, Inc., Publishers

All rights reserved

Copyright, ©, 1964 by Macfadden-Bartell Corporation

New Preface copyright, ©, 1965 by Frederick A. Praeger, Inc.

Library of Congress Catalog Card Number: 65-15692

Printed in the United States of America

The original paperback edition of this book was
published as a Macfadden Capitol Hill Book by the
Macfadden-Bartell Corporation, New York

320.51
M127 L

CONTENTS

21483

PREFACE TO THE NEW EDITION

WHEN I WROTE this book, *A Liberal Answer to the Conservative Challenge*, I anticipated that the campaign of 1964 would be in the tradition of American politics. The campaign just ended, however, was not a "politics as usual" campaign, since the issues were drawn on a different scale and even the language of political discussion was changed.

The men who spoke in 1964 in the name of the Republican Party and of conservatism broke with the traditions of both Republicanism and conservatism. They openly asserted that they spoke with a new voice and proclaimed their intention to offer the voters a clear choice between right and wrong, between good and bad, between absolute success and complete failure.

The attack of Senator Goldwater and of his supporters was not directed primarily at the Democratic Party, but rather at the main movement of American political life. It was an attack against programs and policies accepted in greater or lesser degree by both parties—programs and policies which had been developed to meet the needs of a changing America, programs and policies which had served the needs of America well and which, in new and changing circumstances, had given vitality to the fundamental principles of American economic, social, and political life.

The Republican candidate, Senator Goldwater, stood aside from the three great decisions of the last Congress, decisions involving intellectual, moral, and political commitment: the test-ban treaty, civil rights, and the complex of programs to move the American economy and meet the material needs of Americans. The debate in the campaign, therefore, was not the liberal-conservative debate which I had anticipated and hoped for. There was, in fact, no debate. The Goldwater case was a case against history—a radical one which did violence to the structure of American society, government, and politics.

It cast suspicion on legislative action already taken by the federal government.

It suggested that the federal government was the enemy of the people and of freedom.

It dismissed the complicated problems of poverty, automation, and other changes in the American economy and American society as temporary conditions which nature or providence could take care of, and suggested as a solution a return to methods which had been ineffective in the past when applied to less complicated problems and at a time when change was less rapid than it is today. As James Reston said, those who made this case trifled with most serious things, including the most serious of all things in this century—the matter of war and peace.

On November 3, the people of the country spoke decisively in rejecting this extreme approach. The voice of the electorate was not just a Democratic voice, but expressed the judgment of Republicans and independents as well. It was not just a liberal voice, but one in which liberals and conservatives joined in rejecting the departure from the traditional politics of America.

The interrupted debate between the liberal and the conservative approach can now be resumed. What I have written in this book, I believe, is again relevant to American political discussion and controversy.

EUGENE J. MCCARTHY

November, 1964

6

THE BANNER YET WAVES

IN THE YEARS since the end of World War II, the decline if not the passing of liberalism has been noted and commented on by liberals, conservatives, and neutrals, in the press and on public platforms.

Immediately after the war, the commentaries were, for the most part, by friends of liberalism like Joseph C. Harsch who, in the September 1952 issue of *The Reporter*, suggested that time had run out on the liberals and they were in danger of becoming obsolete. About a year later, in the June 1953 issue of the same magazine, Eric Goldman called upon liberals to rethink their position and to do this "amid the shock of losing the old landmarks and more than a little hand-wringing defeatism."

Conservatism reportedly was rising in the meantime; after the second Eisenhower victory it was said to hold the high ground. Conservatives then asserted quite boldly that they had captured what they called the "American consensus," and were standing firmly astride the "authentic American center."

The warnings, the admonitions, and the suggestions of men like Harsch and Goldman were in order in 1952 and 1953. War, the passage of time, and the changes that had taken place during the war and were taking place in the postwar period called for new thought and new action. But the claims of conservatives as to their gains and positions of positive power were and are subject to serious question.

What liberals have been driven from the field? What kind of liberalism has been displaced?

Liberals come in many varieties. There are pure liberals, self-styled liberals, avowed liberals, and pseudoliberals—to give only the principal labels. There is the liberalism of the 19th century, the liberalism of John Dewey, the liberalism of Reinhold Niebuhr, the liberalism of the New Deal, the liberalism of Adlai Stevenson. There are those called liberals by William Buckley, conservative editor of the *National Review*, who do "not know how to think" in an "enormous area" and who are "inconsistent," "illogical," and "unable to assess evidence." There are the liberals feared by Russell Kirk, who are "rationalists" and lacking in "trust in Providence." Some of these, undoubtedly, have left the field of combat; some have retired, some have been left behind, some were rejected, some defeated—but not all.

The object of this book is to determine whether there is an authentic American liberalism today and to assess it as a force and power in American politics and life.

This task would be much easier if there were an established and clear definition of liberalism. In the absence of that, it might be well to forbid the use of the word "liberalism" as a noun and allow only the use of the adjective "liberal." Under this practice, no one could be simply a *liberal*; he would be a liberal something. Anyone who was called a liberal could demand an answer to the question, "A liberal what?" and insist that the adjective be associated with at least one substantive.

In religion one could not be simply a liberal, but would be a liberal Baptist, a liberal Anglican, a liberal Catholic, or a liberal of some other denomination. In politics he would be a liberal Republican, a liberal Democrat, or a liberal Vegetarian.

Debate without careful and adequate definition of terms may have at least two undesirable results. It may keep people from discussing basic issues because of lack of agreement over definition and it may prevent them from discussing serious practical problems which exist with or without definitions.

The current liberal-conservative debate has in some ways been distracting. It has resulted in name-calling and unwarranted attribution of characteristics. Liberals have been accused of being materialists—conservatives of believing in economic determinism; liberals of lacking faith—conservatives of having no trust in human reason; liberals of perpetuating and sharpening the class struggle—conservatives of advocating unlimited competition, the survival of the fittest as the dynamic of life and progress in society.

To say that liberalism is not what its critics say it is, or, at least, that they cannot prove it to be so, is to contribute little; neither would another definition of conservatism added to the many already offered by both conservatives and liberals be especially useful.

8

American liberalism is not a particular system of philosophy or of theology. It is not a school of political, economic, or social thought. It is not, as some claim, and as some charge, a "way of life." It is not a "demanding faith," as the Americans for Democratic Action assert, although it does make some demands on its adherents. It is not an "undemanding faith," as it has been described by Professor William Leuchtenburg of Harvard, nor is it without faith or without a "home for faith," as it has been said to be by Dr. Frederick Wilhelmsen of Santa Clara University.

What then is American liberalism?

Is it a purely practical response to current needs or pressures, or does it have a basis in ideas?

American liberalism of the second half of the 20th century is not simply a continuation of the liberalism of the 18th or of the 19th centuries. It retains some of the content, the ideals, and the goals of the New Deal, but these have been changed and adjusted to new conditions.

Liberals have not abandoned problems of political economy (as Joseph Harsch suggested they do), for many such problems remain: the economic problems of the aging and of the unemployed, for example. At the same time liberals have in good measure responded in those other areas which Mr. Harsch suggested need attention—education, for instance, and the defense of liberty in such areas as censorship, loyalty proceedings, security firings, picketing and assembly, and criminal proceedings relative to *habeas corpus*. They have not been unmindful of other things on Joseph Harsch's list: special problems of local or nonfederal corruption, exploitation, and injustice; efficient and fair administration of the law; and proper management of our resources.

The quantitative liberalism of the New Deal has persisted, but the qualitative liberalism asked for by Arthur Schlesinger, Jr. is also being demonstrated.

American liberalism has its roots in the ideas that underlie the Declaration of Independence and the Constitution. The ideas upon which 20th century liberalism is based are those of which G. K. Chesterton wrote after visiting the United States: "America is the only nation in the world that is founded on a creed. That creed is set forth with dogmatic and even theological lucidity in the Declaration of Independence; perhaps the only piece of practical politics that is also theoretical politics and also great literature." The creed, as stated in the Declaration, is this: ". . . that all Men are created equal, that they are endowed by their Creator with certain unalienable Rights, that among these are Life, Liberty, and the Pursuit of Happiness—That to secure these

9

Rights, Governments are instituted among Men, deriving their just Powers from the Consent of the Governed. . . ."

We should add to this the classic statement of the purposes of government set forth in the Preamble to the Constitution: ". . . to form a more perfect union, establish justice, insure domestic tranquility, provide for the common defence, promote the general welfare, and secure the blessings of liberty to ourselves and our posterity. . . ." And add also the affirmation of belief in the dignity of man contained in the First Amendment and in other sections of the Bill of Rights.

The basic ideas or concepts are these: self-determination, equality, liberty, and the positive role of government. Of these four basic concepts the only one subject to serious debate is the last—that of the role of government. It is on this point that liberals and conservatives in the United States come closest to ideological or doctrinaire—as well as practical—disagreement. The other ideas are generally accepted by both liberals and conservatives.

We are today in the concluding phase of the controversy over equality. This is not the concluding phase of debate but of controversy, for the debate was settled long ago. The idea of equality as a moral, religious, and philosophical principle was given political substance in the Declaration of Independence. This document requires the acceptance of the idea that each man is by his nature equal in dignity to all other men and that, for this reason, he demands respect. Nothing accidental in individual men takes away this basic dignity: neither race, color, physical stature, nor cultural differences give anyone assured advantages in society or before the law.

The second basic idea is that of liberty. Liberty, too, is recognized and endorsed by both liberals and conservatives. Following this idea—or consistent with it, or arising from it —is the idea of limited government and the protection of areas of free choice and individual decision. In practice it is reflected in the continuing effort to strike a balance or reasonable compromise between individual liberty and the demands of the common good.

This is a historic area of conflict, an area in which lines cannot always be as clearly drawn as in dealing with equality. The liberty of one man may be the restraint of another. In the name of liberty restrictive actions are taken against some. In the name of liberty positive action to insure the exercise of free choice is often taken. In the name of liberty freedom of speech and of worship are claimed. In the name of liberty restrictive ordinances are passed and laws restraining and punishing criminals are justified.

10

The third basic idea is that of the right to life. This right is unchallenged in American politics, except in those cases when it is forfeited because of criminal actions.

The differences between American liberals and American conservatives are not over acceptance of these basic ideas or dedication to their realization. The differences are rather of application and of attitude.

There are two broad areas of political decision calling for attention and action in the U. S. today. One is the field of human rights, which involves the rights of our own people as well as those of people in other countries; the second is that of economic and social justice.

Basically, what is involved in social justice is production of goods adequate to meet the needs of people, and a system or method of ownership and of participation in production through which a claim to a share in the distribution is established.

Paul Henri Spaak, the executive secretary of the North Atlantic Treaty Organization, summarized the full significance of these two obligations in addressing the North Atlantic Community Conference in September, 1957, when he said: "There can be no respect of persons if there is no political democracy and there can be no respect of persons without social justice, and only when we have carried this to its maximum, not only in our own countries but also in all places where we have undertaken political responsibilities, shall we find ourselves in a state of quiet conscience and moral peace which will allow us genuinely to take up the challenge of communism."

If the conservatives have a better response to this challenge, now is the time for them to demonstrate it in word and in action. It is not enough to declare for freedom, truth, and justice, or to declare even more vaguely for traditional values and against an inadequately defined "liberalism."

It is certain that the totality of contemporary thought and contemporary problems cannot be fully or adequately separated and classified under the terms "liberalism" and "conservatism." Yet it is under these banners—pale and tattered —that much of the debate in politics, economics, education, and art is being carried on. There is not enough time to change the flags. We must proceed, hoping that clarification and understanding may be reached along the way.

Part I

THE SCALES OF
ECONOMIC JUSTICE

☆☆☆ *Chapter 1*
TAXES AND THE QUEST FOR EQUITY

The principles of sound taxation have not changed very much since they were stated by Adam Smith in 1776. A sound tax system, he said, should raise enough revenue; it should be just; it should be easy to administer; and it should stimulate economic growth.

On these principles there is general agreement between liberals and conservatives. However, significant differences exist in practice.

There is no simple or ultimate solution. Tax laws will continue to include compromises—some of them undoubtedly political, but most of them reflecting differences in opinions on economic and social good. There will be continuing argument over the effect of taxation on business and on economic growth. Changing social patterns will require adjustments relating to marital status, children, conditions of health and age, standards of education, and charitable and religious activities. Negative or social control objectives will continue to be reflected in our tax laws, as they are today in excise taxes levied on such things as liquor, tobacco, and gambling. Special needs of the government for revenue—particularly in times of war—must bear importantly upon tax programs.

The progressive income tax is a special target of the conservatives. Some even advocate the repeal of the 16th Amendment. This objective is embodied in a pending resolution which proposes an amendment to the Constitution of the United States that would abolish the personal income, estate, and gift taxes and prohibit the United States from engaging in business in competition with its citizens. A somewhat

13

more moderate approach is that recommended in legislation providing for a gradual and scheduled reduction of the income tax rates.

Many conservatives oppose the corporate tax rate on the grounds that it has a depressing effect on the economy, or that it is double taxation. Conservatives have generally advocated tax provisions favoring unearned income such as interest and dividends, or offering special concessions, such as those included in stock options, pension contributions, depletion allowances, and special capital gains treatment.

There is no one, simple rule that can be applied to each of these special forms of taxation or tax exemption. Each must be examined in the context of the business and financial structure to which it applies.

It is most difficult in the field of taxation to determine exactly what constitutes justice and equity. The basic rights of all citizens are equal, but when government action reaches beyond insuring equality before the law into the more complex problems of providing services and imposing obligations, allowance must be made for individual differences and inequalities. Distributive justice, the obligation of public officials toward citizens, requires that obligations and benefits be assigned on a proportionate basis rather than on one of absolute equality.

An absolutely equal application, as Aristotle noted, would itself involve injustice. "But this is the origin of quarrels and complaints," he said, "when either equals have or are awarded unequal shares; or unequals, equal shares." This principle is involved most directly in debates over the progressive rates of the federal income tax.

Although there is a continuing debate even among liberals as to whether the rates themselves are proper or defensible, it is generally accepted by liberals that tax rates should reflect in some degree the taxpayer's ability to pay; that is, the rate should be higher for those in high income brackets. The top rate in the federal income tax scale has been, for many years, 91 percent. Few taxpayers actually pay this rate on all of their income. Some derive income from tax-exempt bonds. Many benefit from special dividend credits and deductions now provided in the law. Many have changed their investments so as to be able to take advantage of the capital gains provisions of the law.

In the case of the personal income tax, the argument is made that the reduction or removal of such taxes would increase purchasing power, stimulate savings, and arouse the initiative of the worker or the entrepreneur. In almost every case those who pay a particular tax argue that the whole economy would benefit if that tax were removed.

If what is under consideration is an excise tax, the argument is made that its removal would release purchasing power, stimulate production, increase corporate profits and subject more individual income to taxation. If what is under consideration is a corporate profits tax, the argument is made that its removal would lower prices, stimulate industry, increase dividends, and encourage savings and reinvestment; and that because of one or another of these changes, or a combination of them, the removal of this tax would increase governmental revenue from other sources.

Liberals and conservatives in some confusion argue for exceptions and against inequities. Once an exception is established, the tendency is to extend it. Lawyers and tax advisers are quick to seize upon any opening in the laws which gives them an argument for asking "most favored" treatment for an industry or a client. The theory seems to be that to take an inequity and extend it so as to make it universal is to establish justice. Each new exception is likely to arouse demands for additional exceptions or exemptions and often results in making the tax laws more complicated and more difficult to enforce.

This is quite clearly the problem with regard to capital gains treatment of income, and depletion allowances. Not all capital gains tax treatment should be considered as a "loophole." If favorable treatment has a direct, reasonable, desired economic or social objective, it may be defended. Under the provisions of the law today, income which qualifies as capital gain, and which results fom the sale of an asset held by an individual for longer than six months, is reduced by one-half for tax purposes and is then taxed at a maximum rate of only 50 percent. This results in an effective tax rate of 25 percent.

This law has long been justified on the grounds that it stimulates new investment, or "risk-taking," and that it frees investors from being locked into current investments. There are some who argue that the present effective rate of 25 percent should be further reduced, or the tax eliminated wholly, in order to set investments free.

The advantage in capital gains lies not only in the differential in rates between that and ordinary individual income rates, but in the fact that in many cases the capital gains tax is not collected. Professor Harold M. Groves, in a report to the Ways and Means Committee of the House of Representatives in November 1959, observed that, "Probably the most serious unneutrality in our present tax treat-

15

ment of capital gains is its failure to reach more than a minor fraction of such gains due to retention of investments through the life of the investor and the tax forgiveness of such gains at death." The inheritor of the property might, if not subject to inheritance tax, sell the property and pay no tax at all.

Capital gains treatment has been extended to more and more forms of income. Once applied principally to real estate and investments in permanent structures, it has now been extended to include profits on sales of stocks and bonds, royalties on coal and timber, and livestock sales under certain conditions. One of the most famous Treasury rulings was that whereby the lump sum sale of General Eisenhower's book, *Crusade in Europe*, for $625,000 was ruled to be a capital gains transaction rather than one involving ordinary individual income.

Since 1954, the first $50 of dividend income has been excluded from taxable income and four percent of dividend income may be taken as a credit against taxes. The principal arguments made for these provisions at the time of their adoption were: First, double taxation would be reduced, namely the levying of corporate income taxes and individual income taxes on the same income; and second, additional investment would be encouraged.

In his 1961 tax message to the Congress, President Kennedy recommended that the present dividend exclusion and dividend credit provisions of the Internal Revenue Code be repealed. The Congress did not follow this recommendation in its tax reform measures. The Administration tax bill of 1963 also proposed the elimination of this provision in the law.

For the "double taxation" argument to be at all tenable, it is necessary that two conditions be fulfilled: One, that the corporate income tax is not shifted to the consumer in the form of higher prices; and two, that the price at which shareholders purchase their stock does not reflect a discount of future expected tax payments. Evidence indicates that both assumptions are open to question and, on the basis of what we now know, provides shaky grounds for the "double taxation" argument.

According to the 1959 *Statistics of Income*, published by the Department of the Treasury, taxpayers with adjusted gross incomes of $10,000 or more filed about 8 percent of all tax returns but accounted for 76 percent of all dividends reported after exclusion. Since there is evidence that "double taxation" is in itself a questionable term, and since there is no proven relationship between dividend credit and exclusion

16

and either investment incentives or the rate of economic growth, the granting of special tax treatment does not seem justifiable.

Another special provision in the tax law which has been subject to severe criticism is the provision for depletion allowances. These allowances were first made available to the oil industry to encourage exploration and expansion of the industry in the interest of national defense. In the years since this first concession, almost every extractive industry has appeared before the Congress to petition for somewhat similar treatment. Each argues that it must meet special needs. Depletion allowances are granted not only to oil and coal and other minerals but even to such products as oyster shells, sand and gravel.

Some critics of depletion allowances argue that they no longer encourage development; others, that they overstimulate development and consequently keep the return on investment below what it would be if there were no such allowances. On the other hand, these allowances have been built into the fiscal structures of most extractive industries.

The depletion allowance is subject to challenge on grounds of equity and also on the basis of its possible economic effects. It should be carefully re-examined.

In somewhat the same category is the special tax treatment given through stock options. As Professor Erwin N. Griswold stated to the House Ways and Means Committee: "The provisions of the tax law with respect to stock options are of substantial benefit to a very few taxpayers. The fact that these provisions are obscure and rarely used may enhance their attractiveness to those who use them; economic gain that one can obtain for his efforts without much specific publicity and without paying any tax can be very satisfactory indeed."

Stock options are inherently discriminatory. They can be and ordinarily are limited to one employee or to a few employees. If the stock is sold, then it may be taxed, but the income realized on the sale of this stock is taxed as a capital gain. If the stock is simply held until death, there is no income tax at any time, no matter how much the actual gain may have been.

The gain prior to the exercise of the option is not really a capital gain. An employee who has a stock option has no capital investment before the option is exercised. He has risked nothing and he loses nothing if the value of the stock goes down. When prices go up, he can exercise his option and get a substantial benefit without current taxation and very likely without ever paying any income tax.

On the other hand when prices go down, he can, with a little difficulty, get a new option at the lower price and may realize a much larger gain later, again without current taxation and with the prospect of paying no income tax at all.

Stock options are least effective in small companies where their use might be most easily justified. In smaller companies, where the efforts of an individual can have some impact on the value of the stock, and where an outsider brought in to improve the management can, through a stock option, share in the improvement of the company, the determination of the fair market value of the stock at any particular date is most difficult and uncertain.

Taken all together, the principal justification for the stock option seems to be its use as a device to reduce the effects of high personal income tax rates. This in itself is insufficient justification for such a discriminatory provision.

Equity in the tax structure must be sustained by equitable and effective administration of the law. Since the income tax is the basic source of federal revenue and since it incorporates the principle of progressive taxation, it is vitally important that the integrity of the tax be protected.

An argument can be made that some forms of income should be treated differently from ordinary income on which the progressive rate is applied. Such things as length of investment, measure of risk involved, and the use to which the invested income is put should be considered. Yet each such exception raises serious questions and requires most careful examination.

While our federal tax structure is not without some weaknesses, and while one must admit that it contains some inequities, it is considerably better than the tax systems of many other countries and generally superior to state and local systems. There is, of course, need for improvement and for continuous review and modification to meet changes in government and in the business and financial practices of the nation.

To safeguard the tax structure, three things are vitally necessary: First, that inequities in the law be removed insofar as possible; second, that laws be drafted to establish clearly the obligation of the taxpayer; and third, that there be adequate and effective administration. These are objectives on which members of Congress—liberals and conservatives—as well as the executive branch of the government must concentrate.

☆☆☆ *Chapter 2*
MYTHS OF FEDERAL FINANCING

The United States is currently engaged in a very important discussion of economic and fiscal policy. President Kennedy opened this discussion when he made what, to some people, was the rather shocking suggestion that the President of the United States be given some discretionary power to adjust tax rates within limits and thereby to make adjustments in the amount of revenue which the federal government would collect from the taxpayers.

This suggestion was new, but not revolutionary, when you consider that the President already has limited authority to make adjustments in trade and tariff policies, including both duties and quotas. He has some discretionary authority in the handling of the public debt and, directly and indirectly, he has some influence upon interest policies in the United States.

Theoretically, of course, the Federal Reserve System is independent. The Supreme Court may not follow the elections, as Mr. Dooley said it did—there are some members of Congress who say it runs ahead of the elections—but the Federal Reserve System does seem to follow the elections. The President has some discretionary authority over the rate of federal spending. In 1963 the President asked for discretionary authority to cut taxes, but urged the Congress itself to cut taxes in order to stimulate economic growth and expansion.

It is not my intention to take up the economic arguments. My hope is rather that as a kind of preliminary to such basic arguments, I may clear away some of the misunderstanding, and cut away the underbrush so that the real woodsmen may come in to get at the trees.

There are three widely and strongly held conservative ideas which bear importantly upon this discussion: One, that a balanced budget is an ultimate good; two, that absolute control of inflation is not only an economic good but also a moral good; and three, that government expenditures by their very nature are wasteful and noneconomic.

In former times it was not unusual for the head of a state to carry a moral theologian as a consultant. Today most heads of state, including even Charles de Gaulle, have economic advisors. A strong case could be made for having

19

heads of state attended by both economic and moral advisors today. In any case, as one attempts to consider the three propositions to which I have referred, it is almost as important to be prepared to defend oneself against moral charges as it is to be prepared to defend oneself against economic arguments.

I must, therefore, make it clear that liberals are not in any absolute or moral sense in favor of unbalanced budgets; that liberals are not in any absolute or moral sense in favor of inflation—either galloping or creeping—and that liberals do not believe that governmental expenditures are never wasteful. Each of these propositions must be judged in the total context of the needs of the country and, therefore, related to the questions of war and peace and to the movement and condition of the economy, both domestic and international.

A balanced budget may be good or it may be bad. In every national campaign, and in most state and local ones, the condition of the budget or the budget record, both absolute and relative, is an issue. There is no consistency in the pattern of arguments. An administration may claim that it has balanced the budget in three years out of five, or in four years out of seven, or in five out of eight, or in a majority of the years during which it was in power. An administration may argue that it has balanced the budget in more years out of a given number than did the opposition when it was in power. It may claim to have balanced the budget over the cycle or, to use a term recently developed —one which has not been fully explained—that it will achieve a "constructive balance." A party may argue that it has reduced the size of the national debt, or slowed down the rate of debt increase, or it may simply point to the fact that it has balanced the budget or is in the process of balancing the budget in the current year—an election year, if this is the case.

One of the greatest efforts of this kind was made by the Eisenhower Administration in the election years of 1958 and 1960. The budget deficit for fiscal year 1959 was, as all faithful Democrats know, the largest peacetime deficit in the history of the country. This record achievement was made in part by pushing expenditures which might have been made in 1958, an election year, into the budget for 1959 and then moving over to 1960 and pushing expenditures which should have been made in that year, also an election year, into the same 1959 budget. The administration did manage a surplus of about a billion dollars in

20

1960, but this in itself did not insure a Republican victory in the election of that year.

If the political case for a balanced or an unbalanced budget is not clear, neither is the economic one. Between 1947 and 1952, during the years of the Truman Administration, the budget was roughly in balance in four out of six years. The national debt in that period was reduced by about $10 billion. If an over-all balanced budget, or a surplus budget, were an absolute deterrent to economic expansion, this should have been a period of stagnation, if not of economic decline. The record is to the contrary.

In the years from 1953 to 1960—the Eisenhower Administration—the budget was unbalanced in five out of eight years, and the national debt increased by roughly $20 billion. Again, if unbalanced budgets were certain to cause economic growth and economic expansion, these should have been years of significant growth, yet this was not the case.

If increased government expenditures were the key to economic expansion, these should have been years of unparalleled growth, for the total expenditures during the Eisenhower Administration—some $650 billion—were greater than the total of all expenditures by the United States government in the entire history of the country up to that time, if we exclude from the total the wartime years of 1943, 1944, and 1945.

It is sometimes suggested that we ought to apply to federal financing the same standards that we apply in business and in the handling of household budgets. This argument is usually made without much reflection: first of all, because governmental financing is generally not comparable to personal and business financing; and secondly because, on the record, federal financing has been more conservative and more restrained in recent years than has been most personal or domestic financing and most business financing.

Consumer credit in this country, for example, increased from $31 billion to over $63 billion between 1953 and 1962; home mortgages increased in the same period from $63 billion to $168 billion; in roughly the same period, industrial credit increased from about $150 billion to over $227 billion. The increase in federal debt from about $266 billion to $298 billion in the same period was in no way comparable.

Deficit financing and the extension of credit are vital to the American economy. Credit is one of the instruments which have contributed greatly to the growth of Western civilization and certainly to the growth of the United States. Today bankers, who are unanimously in favor of deficit financing in some of its forms at least (since this is an area

21

in which they make their living) are often among those who pronounce a general denunciation of deficit financing when government is involved. Even the Puritans, whose ethic has become a part of the controversy on deficit financing, borrowed money to come to the United States. And Columbus, after trying to raise funds from private sources, financed his trip with a government loan—a kind of Spanish reconstruction finance project.

A popular position on the part of the conservatives is that the imposition of a federal debt ceiling will result in something called "fiscal responsibility." This claim is not supported by the record.

When the debt ceiling was first established, it was claimed that it would make for fiscal responsibility, a balanced budget, and a general increase in the integrity of the federal budget, and that it would make both Congress and the executive branch of the government more responsible. The record of experience under the debt ceiling limitation has not proved any of these claims and, in some cases, the effect has really been the opposite of what it was claimed it would be.

Of course, some partisan politics was involved in the first action to establish the debt ceiling, and some discussions relating to proposed increases in recent years have not been above partisanship. It is customary for conservatives to point out that debt ceilings have been raised under Democratic administrations. But in recent years when Republican administrations were in control of the Treasury, Democrats did not refrain from raising the question as the Republican administration repeatedly came before the Congress asking for either permanent or temporary increases in the national debt ceiling.

I will not attempt to trace the history of the debt limit or to go into the record of party positions relative to it, but rather to discuss some of the serious consequences of the establishment of this arbitrary ceiling.

One of the most serious consequences is that the existence of the debt ceiling has served as an excuse, perhaps justified by necessity, for highly questionable budget practices. These practices have taken several forms. In 1953 the Commodity Credit Corporation, at the request of the Treasury, undertook to finance its own operations by direct operation in the money market. In the second half of 1953 the CCC sold $1.2 billion worth of certificates of interest in the surplus commodities held by the United States government. This amount was not included in the national debt, and $1 billion still outstanding on June 30th of that year disappeared from the 1954 federal budget. When the remainder of the 1953 support loans matured in 1954, bringing much of this back into the budget, approximately the same amount was again financed through certificates of interest.

A similar practice was followed by the Federal National Mortgage Association, which issued in 1955 about a half billion dollars of notes directly to the public. In this case the collateral was the Federal National Mortgage Association portfolio. In each case the interest costs, and consequently the cost to the taxpayer, were substantially higher than they would have been had the programs been financed by direct Treasury obligations.

Again in 1958, in order to keep the debt under the limit, various agencies—but particularly the Federal National Mortgage Association—borrowed funds from the public to permit repayment to the Treasury of sums which had been advanced to them. About $1.5 billion of such repayments were made by the Federal National Mortgage Association from February 1957 to March 1958.

Several other proposals, in part motivated by the existence of the debt ceiling, were not carried out because of the opposition of the Congress and the refusal to pass the necessary legislation. The most extreme of these was the proposal to set up an independent authority to finance the proposed highway building program in 1955. The plan was to authorize an independent authority to issue its own "general revenue bonds" to be repaid out of the growth of federal revenue from excise taxes on gasoline and lubricating oils.

This proposal was different from the FNMA and CCC operations in that in each of the other cases the security behind the loan was either surplus crops or the mortgage holdings of the home loan agency. In the case of the highway financing proposal, the repayment was to depend upon future federal revenues.

These practices have had two results: They have increased the cost of financing government operations, and they have resulted in the publication of a budget which was made to look smaller than it actually was. Such publication would probably not have been dared if the excuse of keeping within the debt ceiling had not been present.

Consider a second claim made for the statutory debt ceiling—that it will curb federal spending and eliminate waste. Let us look, for example, at the $802 million sale of FNMA notes outside the debt limit in 1957. Maturing in only eight months, the notes carried an interest rate of 4⅞ percent when the Treasury could have borrowed

23

money directly at 4 percent. In this particular case, a loss of $4,667,000 can be laid directly to the existence of the debt limit.

The cost of other operations made necessary by the debt ceiling cannot be quite as accurately determined. Nonetheless, the record shows quite clearly that its existence has had serious effects upon the management of federal expenditures and upon the scheduling of financial operations. For example, in January 1958, former Treasury Secretary Anderson estimated that the debt as of September 30th would be $271.3 billion and that this required a debt limit of $274.3 billion. In fact the debt was $276.4 billion as of September 30th. Obviously such an error in estimates made necessary a stretch-out of programs in order to keep within the limit. Such adjustments in the handling of amounts running into millions of dollars cannot be accomplished without waste.

As an over-all curb on the growth of federal debt, the ceiling has been even less effective. In a period of prosperity, when cutbacks of government expenditures might make economic sense, increasing revenues nullify any effect that the debt ceiling might have, since the ceiling does not relate to total government expenditures but rather to past and present differences between receipts and expenditures. Thus between fiscal 1955 and fiscal 1957, federal cash expenditures rose from $70.5 billion to $80 billion, but revenues were also rising at the same time. Consequently the debt ceiling was ineffective. In times of recession, on the other hand, the debt ceiling tightens its grip.

A fourth consequence of the existence of the debt ceiling has been demonstrated in certain arbitrary decisions that have been made. *Business Week* of June 20, 1958 asserted that in the second half of 1957 the debt ceiling forced the administration to cut back programs needed for long-term national security, and stated further that the resulting slash in defense expenditures was an important contributing cause of the recession.

What was done, according to reports, was to stretch out production schedules for plane and missile projects, to restrict overtime for defense contracts, to ban installment buying of weapons, and to impose a $38 billion spending ceiling for fiscal 1958 on the Defense Department. From this came the 5 percent reduction in progress payments, an order to contractors to cut payroll costs 5 percent, the Air Force's limitation on monthly payments to contractors (creating new stretch-outs), and finally a 200,000-man cut in the armed forces. A secondary effect of these cutbacks was their perverse effect upon the growing recession of 1957.

24

Actually the debt ceiling is not an instrument for economic stability. It is ineffective in times of prosperity, when revenue is high, and has a dangerous, arbitrary, braking effect during times of recession. It leads to rigidity in debt management and in thinking with regard to government finance and policy. One Secretary of the Treasury after another has borne this out in testimony.

Former Secretary Anderson, testifying before the Ways and Means Committee, said that there was need for more flexibility and for more efficient and economical management of the debt. We have been able to discharge our obligations within the debt limit only by maintaining cash balances which have been distressingly low at times. We have had little or no margin for contingency.

Other devices have been tried through the years. In 1946, for example, the so-called legislative budget was passed. The Congress provided that each year it should enact an over-all ceiling on expenditure appropriations. In the first year of its operation, individual appropriations pierced the House ceiling by $6 billion and the Senate ceiling by nearly $3 billion. Somewhat similar claims were made for the omnibus appropriation bill which was tried several years later.

The obvious conclusion is that the debt ceiling has not been an effective instrument for controlling government expenditures; that it does not present a realistic picture of the actual debt situation of the federal government; that it has resulted in costly financing operations on the part of the government; that it has undermined in part the integrity of the budget; that it has been expensive to the taxpayers; that it sets up a limitation which can have little or no effect in curbing inflation, but can have serious consequences in interfering with proper action to prevent recession; and that it has, at least in the 1957 period, encouraged the Department of Defense to take action which might well have endangered the national security. Yet the conservatives like it.

The second broad area of discussion involves the belief that a tax cut and deficit financing will result in a larger deficit and, therefore, cause inflation. There are competent economists who argue that inflation would not result but, in any case, the prospect of inflation is held by some as sufficient reason for not taking the proposed action. This argument is based upon a mixture of economic and moral considerations. Speakers on the floor of the Senate assert that whereas the greatest external threat to America is communism, the greatest internal threat is inflation.

There must, of course, be monetary stability. The question is not one of uncontrolled inflation, nor even of planned inflation. There is a difference between uncontrolled inflation, planned inflation, and something which can properly be called controlled inflation. The latter involves a free but not unrestrained play of the economic forces which exist in an economy such as ours—an economy which rests to a large extent upon nongovernmental decisions which in most cases are made on the basis of an optimistic anticipation of an expanding economy.

Sumner Slichter, who has a reputation as a somewhat conservative economist, wrote a series of articles in 1959 dealing with this problem. In one of them, appearing in *The New York Times Magazine* for March 8, 1959, he said:

"Suppose that the economy, which is capable of increasing its productive capacity at the rate of 4% a year, were held to a growth of only 2% a year in order to keep the price level steady. At the end of ten years the economy would have a productive capacity more than 26 percentage points less than it would have had at the greater rate of growth. . . .

"Prices in most other important industrial countries have been rising in recent years even faster than in the United States. Betwen 1950 and 1957, for example, the increase in the index of wholesale prices in Britain was more than twice as large as in the United States. In Sweden and Norway it was more than three times as large, in France almost three times as large, in West Germany almost twice as large, in Austria four times as large. . . ."

There are, he pointed out, "also ill-founded fears that creeping inflation will sooner or later become a gallop. Every country in Europe has had creeping inflation during the past ten years. The idea has become pretty well accepted that a continued drop in purchasing power of money is to be expected. And yet in virtually all countries the rise in prices between 1953 and 1957 was considerably less than in the period 1948 to 1952."

He concluded with these words: "Most important of all, people should realize that the alternative to creeping inflation is a fairly substantial amount of chronic unemployment. The problems of creeping inflation are a small price to pay for avoiding the much greater problems of unemployment and a rate of growth that falls far short of our potential."

Absolute stability is not to be accepted in itself as the best and only standard for making economic decisions. The extreme of this limited approach is reflected in an argument made on the floor of the Senate some time ago by a speaker who, in opposing appropriations for medical research, argued that such appropriations would be inflationary and that consequently the value of life insurance policies would be reduced. In a case of this kind, one would have to weigh the value of extending life, even at the cost of some inflation, against the value of survivors' benefits—in other words, the relative advantages to the principal or to the beneficiary.

Eliot Janeway said recently: "I have no confidence in the confidence of businessmen. I trust the pressures which prod them to action and not the emotions which distract them." This may well be too harsh a judgment, but in any case it points to the fact that pressure can have significant results.

In the case of limited inflation, there are two possible effects: One, that it will encourage people to borrow in anticipation of being able to pay back with dollars which are not worth quite as much as those borrowed—this is on the attractive or encouraging side for those who seek to borrow; on the other hand, there is a kind of pressure which urges people to invest and to use their money and their capital in a productive way rather than simply standing still and expecting money alone to be productive.

The third general point to be considered is the idea that governmental expenditures are essentially unnecessary and wasteful. This is reflected in a number of slogans such as "pork barrel," "feeding at the public trough," and so forth.

There are some governmental expenditures which are undoubtedly wasteful—some because of poor decisions or poor management, and others because of changes in conditions and times. Weapons in the process of being developed may become obsolete even before they become operational.

The same thing can be said about some efforts undertaken by private enterprise. There have been some model failures in the automobile industry; one recent example is the Ford Motor Company's Edsel. About the time the model was to be put on the market, it was said that the car had been designed to meet a special need in American society. The car was, it seems, designed for those who were on the way up but were not quite sure they were going to make it to the top, and also for those who were on the way down but did not want anyone to know it, and possibly, also, for those who had given up. The car did not sell well.

A recent press report made reference to a public statement by one of my Senate colleagues who had criticized a number of projects which had been approved by the National Institutes of Health. Among the projects were such things as a study of the oral health of the Icelandic people, the information contained in echoes, studies in silent thinking, measurement of the beagle brain, and so forth. Judging only by the titles, these seem to be rather ridiculous projects. But, in fact, the oral health of the Icelandic people has special

27

significance in the effort to control dental disease; the information contained in echoes may be of significant help in aiding the blind; the study of the brain of the beagle may be very helpful in brain surgery on human beings. One must look beyond the title.

On November 2, 1900, the *Washington Post* carried a long and powerful editorial which stated: "Of all the silly and nonsensical rigmarole about yellow fever that has yet found its way into print—and there has been enough of it to load a fleet—the silliest beyond compare is to be found in the arguments and theories engendered by the mosquito hypothesis." This was directed at the investigation of the mosquito hypothesis being conducted by Major Walter Reed.

On February 6, 1901, Major Reed was able to announce proof that mosquitoes were in fact the yellow fever carriers. Not every research project turns out as well as this one did, yet successes of this kind do demand that we exercise some prudence before denouncing all governmental expenditures. What is called for is distinction and separation and choice among projects, some of which are good and necessary, and some nonessential and noneconomic.

Suppose we tried to cut the 1964 budget. Where would we cut it? Appropriations for national defense make up well over half of it. Can we risk defense cuts at this time? The answer would appear to be no.

Two other areas in which cuts have been suggested are those of new construction and agriculture. If cuts amounting to something like $10 to $15 billion in these areas were approved, both the immediate and the long-run effect upon the economy would be depressing.

The same conclusion is reached following analysis of any of the proposed cuts, except those affecting projects some limited parts of which could be defined as wholly wasteful and noneconomic.

An attempt at a balanced budget would result in a sharp slowdown of economic activity and drastically curtailed federal revenues, and could result in a budget deficit at the end of the year which would be greater than if there had been no reduction in federal expenditures. There is no magic in a balanced budget, nor any assurance of economic progress in an attempt to achieve one.

Is a balanced or an unbalanced budget good or bad? The answer must be that neither is economically or morally good or bad in itself, but that each budget must be judged in relation to the whole pattern of facts and conditions and forces. To oversimplify and to misapply slogans is to do a

28

disservice to the whole decision-making process in a democracy.

In commenting upon the readiness in Western civilization to say that in every difficult situation a practical man or a practical judgment is needed, G. K. Chesterton said that when the world or civilization is in an impracticable muddle, in addition to practical minds you need minds which deal in theory, which deal in ideas. He added, "It is the why and the how which have to be considered when we are tracing out the way in which some culture or some tradition has got into a tangle."

We need both practical minds and those which deal in theory as we wrestle with contemporary fiscal and economic policies.

It has become more or less respectable in the United States to accept the Keynesian theory that governmental expenditures or governmental deficits can offset or reverse recessions. The suggestion, however, that such expenditures or deficits might be used to move the economy from a relatively stable level of operation to a higher one is looked upon by some as an economic heresy. It is as though, in the field of physics, we continued to insist that only the theories of Newton be applied. To accept that we are condemned to a kind of closed economic cycle is to set our sights too low and to fail to appreciate our potential for economic growth and progress.

What the President and his advisors have suggested is that without a recession, at a time when the economy has leveled off at a relatively high level, it might be possible through deficit financing—in this instance through tax cuts—to move the economy from that high level to a higher one without the intervention of a recession or of a serious falling-off in production.

☆☆☆ *Chapter 3*
THE COMMON STAKE

"Get the government out of business," is a popular conservative political slogan. Of course, those who raise this cry do, when hard pressed, make many reservations and exceptions.

The federal government has been actively involved in the business and economic life of the country since the beginning of our national existence. Between January 1790 and the end of December, 1791, Alexander Hamilton, the first Secretary of the Treasury, presented to the Congress of the newly established United States four reports on fiscal and economic policy.

The first dealt with public credit; it recommended funding the national debt and assuming and funding state debts at par. The second and third concerned themselves with public finance and with private credit, and proposed the incorporation of a national bank and the levying of an excise tax directly on the producers of spirits. The fourth dealt with manufacturing and the tariff, and proposed the establishment of a protective tariff.

Hamilton's proposals were vigorously opposed. This opposition resulted in the organization of the first major political party in the United States—the Jeffersonian Republicans. The issues of government fiscal policy, of credit and interest rates, rates of economic growth, taxes, tariffs, and of government relation to business remain political issues today, not only during campaigns but between them.

There is bound to be tension between government and business, since American business is primarily motivated by search for profit and individual or corporate advancement, and cannot be expected to respond to all of the demands of a broad social or economic nature—demands which require greater attention to the overriding concept of the common good. Government, on the other hand, has primary responsibility for the common good and, therefore, must assert itself when private interests seriously threaten or interfere with the efforts to achieve it.

Government participates in the economic life of the nation both directly and indirectly. Under the general authority of the "welfare clause" of the Constitution and the more clearly stated authority of Section 8 of Article I of the same document, the federal government is charged specifically with responsibility for coining money and regulating its value, levying taxes, and borrowing for the government. These general responsibilities and powers are accepted by both liberals and conservatives. The disagreements arise more often over the interpretation and the application of these powers.

Primarily through regulation, government exercises some control over business and over the economic life of the nation without directly participating in this activity. Regulatory powers serve a number of purposes: They may protect the public, insure a free competitive economy, or promote business activity.

Most of the work of regulation is carried out through

various commissions—the Interstate Commerce Commission, which has responsibility primarily in the field of transportation; the Federal Power Commission, which has limited jurisdiction over the fuel and power supplies of the United States; the Federal Communications Commission, obviously dealing with communications; the Federal Aviation Agency; and so on.

In addition to acting through commissions, the federal government also acts under general statutes such as antitrust legislation, the Taft-Hartley and other labor laws, and the Pure Food and Drug Act.

Substantive government participation in business in the United States is, for the most part, auxiliary. Some industries are subsidized directly, as in the case of the shipping industry and the airlines; some are subsidized indirectly, as is the publishing industry generally through postal service rates which do not meet costs. Small businesses are helped through the Small Business Administration and through special set-asides in defense contracts. The agricultural industry of the country has the help of various credit programs, the Rural Electrification Administration, price support legislation, and programs for the disposal of agricultural production both domestically and abroad.

Direct participation of the government in business and economic activity in the United States is very limited. The Bureau of Reclamation is, I suppose one would say, in the power business, along with its work in irrigation, reclamation, flood control, and navigation. The Tennessee Valley Authority is a government-established corporation which conducts economic activities.

However, the major areas of decision, the major responsibility for the business and economic life of the country, rest with nongovernmental agencies and institutions. Historically the United States governmental policy with reference to business has been one of "watchful waiting." Almost without exception, federal intervention in the economic life of the nation has followed abuse of privilege, or neglect or failure on the part of extra-governmental institutions or individuals to meet the needs of the country.

The record of American business and industry in meeting these needs has generally been good. Certainly the responses to wartime demands were excellent. The one great failure, the depression of the Thirties, must, I think, be attributed to economic and historical forces which businessmen of that period could not in all fairness have been expected to anticipate or to prevent.

Great projects involving multiple purposes, such as the

31

Tennessee Valley Authority and the great hydro-electric power, irrigation, and reclamation projects in the West, are of such nature that extensive public or governmental participation is, of necessity, required. One can raise a serious question as to why the electric power industry of the United States did not respond to the rural power needs of the country more effectively. If it had, the REA as a government-supported program might not have been necessary. Certainly the banking industry could have developed its own insurance program before widespread bank failures necessitated the establishment of the Federal Deposit Insurance Corporation. Social Security raises questions of a somewhat different nature.

Each of these programs was the subject of political controversy when first proposed or adopted; some remain controversial. There is no set pattern of response which breaks clearly on the liberal-conservative line.

Liberals may be divided among themselves on some subsidies; so may the conservatives. Differences exist with reference to regulation. Conservatives identified, for example, with water or truck transportation may very well be opposed to the regulation of their own industries but in favor of regulation of railroads. As a general rule, however, the conservatives oppose additional government action, and liberals are more ready to accept such intervention and participation.

In political campaigns it is customary for liberals to charge that government has not done enough for the economy, and for conservatives to charge that the government is attempting to do too much. Thus, in 1952, Republicans described the economy as being on a "treadmill," and blamed the Democratic administration and its program for that condition. The Democrats in 1960 charged that the rate of economic growth in the United States was not what it should or could be and that government policies—or the lack of them, or the negative character of them—were at least in part responsible.

Soon after the election of President Kennedy there was a great deal written about something called the "crisis of confidence" in the business community. This "crisis of confidence" was used to explain the fall of the stock market, the rise in unemployment, and almost every other unfavorable economic indicator that showed along the way at that time.

In the face of the facts, it was rather hard to establish a basis for this "crisis of confidence." President Kennedy had appointed a Republican, Douglas Dillon, as Secretary

32

of the Treasury; he had appointed a Republican, Robert McNamara, as Secretary of Defense; and he had acted to retain William McChesney Martin as Chairman of the Board of Governors of the Federal Reserve System. He proposed a special tax cut through an investment credit, which resulted in tax reductions for business and industry of over $1 billion a year; the Treasury revised the depreciation schedules, thereby providing an additional tax reduction of more than a billion dollars.

With the administration's support the duPont bill was passed and later the communications satellite bill, which placed responsibility for space communications basically in the hands of private enterprise. Inflationary pressures were under control, and the economy itself was operating at a relatively high level—at least there had been no recession. All of these things taken together should have contributed to business confidence, and yet the claim was made that there was a "crisis of confidence."

By Republican and conservative standards the economy in 1963 is doing very well. There has been no recession. Whereas there is some criticism from Republican sources, the most publicized criticism has come from those who would be classified as "liberals."

Leon Keyserling, for example, testifying before the Joint Economic Committee of the Congress on February 17, 1963, had this to say: "I have a natural reluctance to being critical of the President's program, for I admire his elevated purposes, courage, and discernment. Nonetheless, I am convinced that the President's tax proposals miss the mark so widely that it will be useful to set forth my views clearly and with candor, and that this course can be helpful to the President as well as to others. Indeed, I feel that the deficiencies in the President's tax program spring primarily from his sincere reliance upon economic advice which appears to be mistaken, and that he will in due course reappraise this advice when it is shown to work no better in the future than it has worked to date."

In addition, Keyserling criticized the administration's approach to wage problems. It was unduly concentrated, he said, upon the prevention of inflationary wage increases in excess of productivity gains. Keyserling summarized his criticism in these paragraphs:

"(1) Economic policies in government, no less than in business, should be a means rather than an end. In order that the policies be relevant and adequate, the ends must first be stated in terms of meaningful and thorough quantitative targets or end objectives, both long range and short range. The relevant targets, in this instance, are the needed levels of employment, production, and purchasing power, broken down into major components, and projected for a reasonable number of years ahead, with due account of the priorities of our needs, and of needed adjustments in the structure of demand. This the Employment Act of 1946 not only contemplates, but indeed requires. The Council of Economic Advisers, in its current Report, has abandoned even some tentative and fragmentary efforts to do this, which it earlier had commenced.

"(2) The second explanation resides in the artificial dichotomy between economic and social purposes, resulting in two Reports so disappointingly devoid of adequate policies expressly related to these social purposes. It is not enough to say that everybody will be better off, and our social purpose thus served, if our economic performance is improved. For the very nature of our chronic and current economic trouble is that those social programs which add directly to human well-being, which improve the distribution of the fruits of our production, are at the very heart of potentially successful economic efforts.

"After all, the real challenge of the unused resources, resulting from not meeting this problem, is in the form of *opportunity*—the opportunity to eradicate the poverty and deprivation which still afflict two-fifths of our population, and to lift all Americans to decent levels of living compatible with our soaring power to produce; to take millions of families out of slums; to provide them with more educational opportunities and better health services in line with our technical competence to do so; to cleanse their cities and purify their waters; to enlarge their security in their old age; to enable them to be transported more conveniently; to improve the natural resources which will be the heritage of their descendants; and even to enable a larger proportion of them to enjoy the more conventional material comforts of life, and to enjoy more leisure—and not in the form of involuntary unemployment. These are not merely the by-products of a successful economy program; they are an essential and major portion of the

34

implementation of such a program. An economic program which does not recognize this sufficiently will fall far short of economic restoration, because it does not accurately sense the very nature of the task. And it will not rally the American people fully to the task, because it does not come close enough to their most profound needs and aspirations."

This is certainly comprehensive criticism, calling for a comprehensive response. Putting aside the particulars of this statement, the point that comes through is that Mr. Keyserling represents the liberal point of view, at least to this extent: He insists that reasoned judgment be applied to the economy and the business community and to its problems; and that to leave these problems to nature or to the operation of economic laws (which, with some over-simplifications, is called the conservative approach) is to declare for the irrational.

Technical processes, which includes business and economic processes, must be directed to human ends. As times change, new theories and new institutions, or changes in the old, are called for. In our complicated economic society today, it is not only as wrong and useless to put forward the ideas of socialization or of nationalization as it is to argue for absolute free enterprise. Concentrations of economic power today call for a measure of moral control, demanding, therefore, deliberate attention to both freedom and justice.

These are not simply by-products or incidental to other activity, for their attainment, perfection, and preservation require reasoned attention. The idea of "survival of the fittest" does not apply to human society; nor is J. K. Galbraith's theory of "countervailing power" a satisfactory substitute for responsible decision.

W. H. Ferry, in an address to the Danforth Foundation Seminar in Colorado Springs on June 28, 1962, stated the case in these words: "The familiar argument against making justice the regulative principle of the economic order is to say that the economic machine exists principally to produce goods and services for the nation as efficiently as possible. It is always added that the notorious inefficiencies of political direction would ruin economic arrangements."

On the other hand, he says, "democracy means self-government. It means a deliberate focus on freedom and justice. It means continuous concern for personal dignity. . . . A commitment to democracy means a commitment to justice." "Instead," he says, "of thinking and doing something about it—that is to say, being imaginative and moral —we pretend that it [injustice] does not exist; and when woeful conditions accidentally swim before our gaze, we have stock responses, all of them substitutes for thought."

Even more fundamental questions of theory and historical judgment must be admitted. Communists today are repeating the Marxist criticism that the capitalistic system cannot solve the problems of distribution. This is a serious challenge and one which we cannot set aside or leave to the operation of simple laws of economics. Unemployment is disturbingly high. The head of the National Association of Manufacturers recently forecast that by 1970 approximately 10 million people would be unemployed in the United States unless there are changes made. Automation is a fact and its consequences are real. The basis upon which every person should have a share in the production of our economy should be a share or participation in the productive effort of our economy. This must be our concern—the concern of government, of business, of industry: To see that everyone who can work and who will work has an opportunity to do so and, on the basis of that work, has a claim on and a share of the total production.

We must acknowledge, too, that some of the early and simple rules of competition, which work well when there are many small producers competing in a free and open market, do not work as effectively when great concentration of economic power is involved. We must acknowledge that with an increase in power there must be a corresponding increase in responsible control.

Part II

OF PAYROLLS
AND POVERTY

☆☆☆ *Chapter 1*
THE POOR: THEIR PLIGHT
AND RIGHTS

In his book, *The Other America,* Michael Harrington estimates the number of poor in the United States as between 40 and 50 million people. Harrington does not equate poverty with starvation, but points out that "tens of millions of Americans are . . . maimed in body and spirit, existing at levels beneath those necessary for human decency."

One might define poverty so as to cut the number of poor sharply below this estimate, but there is no doubt that poverty is still a fact of life in the United States. There are about 8 million families today with incomes less than $2,500 a year, and another 7 million with incomes between $2,500 and $4,000. In 1958, 14.3 percent of the families and unattached individuals in the United States had incomes of $2,000 a year or less; 10 percent, between $2,000 and $3,000 a year; 12 percent, between $3,000 and $4,000 a year. (*Statistical Abstract,* 1960) Nearly 7 million people depend on public assistance for all or part of the income they must have for basic necessities.

We have 16 million citizens in the United States who are 65 years or over; by 1970 the number will be 20 million. Most of these people have very limited financial means. More than half of the families headed by a person over 65 have annual incomes below $3,000, and four-fifths of all people in this age group who live alone must subsist on less than $2,000 a year.

It is estimated that 14 million American families live in substandard or deteriorating homes. One-third of the 6 million nonwhite households have substandard housing. Two million new homes a year are needed to provide housing for the new family units being formed in the U. S.

Under such conditions, does government have any obligation? The conservative position generally is that it does not; the liberal position is that it does have a responsibility.

The story of Western civilization is in large measure the record of man's efforts to improve and perfect human society. It is a record of individual and personal effort, but also of community and political endeavor. These social and political aspects have been the concern of philosophers and of men of action throughout the centuries: the ancient Greek political thinkers, the Roman jurists, the medieval canonists, the men of the Enlightenment and of the modern world—Plato and Aristotle, Justinian, Thomas Aquinas, Thomas More, Montesquieu, Jefferson, Madison, Hamilton, and a host of contemporary spokesmen.

Concern over poverty and concern for the poor run as a significant theme throughout Western history. In earlier times, poverty was accepted as inevitable, and it was dealt with on an institutional basis.

The forms of response to the needs of the poor, and the motives for that response, have varied. In some cases certain classes or groups of persons have been almost wholly excluded from concern—those of another nation, caste, race, or religion—but no society or civilization has shown total and complete indifference.

The care of the poor is recorded in the Old Testament as having high priority and importance among the Jewish people. In Chapter 15 of the Book of Deuteronomy, the measure of responsibility is defined in these words: "If one of your kinsmen in any community is in need in the land which the Lord your God has given to you, you shall not harden your heart, nor close your hand to him in his need."

In medieval times response to the needs of the poor was considered a personal responsibility. It was accepted also as deserving of organized attention. The care of those in need—physical and intellectual as well as spiritual—was accepted as a special function of the religious orders of the times. Concern for the poor and service in their need was a mark of perfection and of love. The giving of alms was a religious act, not merely an act of human compassion or one demanded by reasoned concern for justice. The voluntary acceptance of poverty was considered as a step toward holiness, and begging achieved some respectability.

It was perhaps inevitable that voluntary agencies could not adequately care for all of the needs, and quite certain that with the development of the modern democratic state,

38

other public bodies would assume a share of responsibility. The process was accelerated in medieval times by the suppression of monasteries and the confiscation of religious properties.

Whatever the reasons or combination of causes, the attitude toward the poor and toward poverty changed in later times. Poverty came to be looked upon increasingly as a mark of personal defect or as a punishment for unknown or unpublished faults.

The extreme 19th century position was stated by Herbert Spencer: "Pervading all nature we may see at work a stern discipline, which is a little cruel that it may be very kind. . . . The poverty of the incapable, the distresses that come upon the imprudent, the starvation of the idle, and those shoulderings aside of the weak by the strong . . . are the decrees of a large, far-seeing benevolence. . . . Similarly, we must call spurious philanthropists, who to prevent a present misery, would entail greater misery upon future generations. All defenders of a poor-law must be classed among them. . . ." (From *Social Statics*)

In the 19th century the philosophy of individualism was strongly held in the United States, although its effects were moderated and mitigated by the closeness of family ties and of community life and by the continuously opening frontier. Poverty was viewed by many as a proper punishment of the derelict and of the wasteful and lazy. The cold threat of being sent to the county poor farm was a warning to provide for one's later years.

Conservatives today take a somewhat less severe position. Senator Goldwater, in his book *The Conscience of a Conservative*, writes: "Let us, then, not blunt the noble impulses of mankind by reducing charity to a mechanical operation of the federal government. Let us, by all means, encourage those who are fortunate and able to care for the needs of those who are unfortunate and disabled. But let us do this in a way that is conducive to the spiritual as well as the material well-being of our citizens—and in a way that will preserve their freedom. Let welfare be a private concern. Let it be promoted by individuals and families, by churches, private hospitals, religious service organizations, community charities and other institutions that have been established for this purpose."

A century ago the 160-acre homestead became the symbol of opportunity and independence, while the city man envisioned ownership of a small plant or shop—something he could call his own and direct and use as he saw fit. This dream lingered, but the reality was something far different.

In a highly industrialized and extremely mobile society such as ours, the old institutions which provided dignity and security no longer were effective, or at least not to the same degree. Government accepted new obligations in its function as protector of the rights and freedom of the individual.

Toward the end of the century, changes began to appear. At first there were laws to curb some of the worst abuses, to provide minimum standards for working conditions for children and women, and later for men as well. The great change occurred during the depression of the Thirties. Quite suddenly the United States found itself with some 14 million persons out of work, with its agricultural economy in a desperate condition, and with business and finance staggered—all without any obvious explanation in terms of sudden moral failure among workers, farmers, and businessmen. There was no opportunity for the eager and ambitious, in the land of opportunity; no bread for millions, in the land of plenty.

The conservative position was reflected in the Republican platform of 1932. Adopted in the midst of the great depression, the party plank on unemployment and relief states: "True to American traditions and principles of Government the administration [President Hoover's] has regarded the relief problem as one of state and local responsibility. . . . The Republican Party . . . is opposed to the Federal Government entering directly into the field of private charity and direct relief to the individual. . . ."

The election of President Roosevelt was followed by a significant national change. It was manifest in governmental programs reflecting the view that government must assume additional responsibility for the economic welfare of the people and, beyond that, for their more general welfare. This, in effect, became the image of the New Deal. President Roosevelt himself, near the completion of his third term, expressed his view of the general relationship between political and economic rights in his State of the Union message of 1944:

> "We cannot be content, no matter how high the general standard of living may be, if some fraction of our people—whether it be one-third or one-fifth or one-tenth—is ill-fed, ill-clothed, ill-housed, and insecure.
>
> "This Republic had its beginning, and grew to its present strength, under the protection of certain

inalienable political rights—among them the right of free speech, free press, free worship, trial by jury, freedom from unreasonable searches and seizures. They were our rights to life and liberty.

"As our Nation has grown in size and stature, however—as our industrial economy expanded— these political rights proved inadequate to assure us equality in the pursuit of happiness.

"We have come to a clear realization of the fact that true individual freedom cannot exist without economic security and independence. 'Necessitous men are not free men.' People who are hungry and out of a job are the stuff of which dictatorships are made.

"In our day these economic truths have become accepted as self-evident. We have accepted, so to speak, a second Bill of Rights under which a new basis of security and prosperity can be established for all, regardless of station, race, or creed.

"Among these are:

"The right to a useful and remunerative job in the industries or shops or farms or mines of the Nation;

"The right to earn enough to provide adequate food and clothing and recreation;

"The right of every farmer to raise and sell his products at a return which will give him and his family a decent living;

"The right of every businessman, large and small, to trade in an atmosphere of freedom from unfair competition and domination by monopolies at home or abroad;

"The right of every family to a decent home;

"The right to adequate medical care and the opportunity to achieve and enjoy good health;

"The right to adequate protection from the economic fears of old age, sickness, accident, and unemployment;

"The right to a good education.

"All of these rights spell security. And after this war is won we must be prepared to move forward, in the implementation of these rights, to new goals of human happiness and well-being."

If we agree that these are rights or needs, it follows that programs are certainly defensible when designed to provide fair and just treatment of workingmen, to insure mini-

41

mum wages, and to protect farmers against loss of income through crop failure and depressed farm prices. It follows, too, that a case can be made for programs to provide a measure of security against the uncertainties of unemployment, of disabling accidents, of sickness and old age, and for legislation to assist families in acquiring adequate housing and adequate education for the children.

These have been the elements of the liberal program and, to the extent that these needs are not met, they remain as essential parts of that program.

☆☆☆ *Chapter 2*
THE REAL RIGHT TO WORK

Unemployment is in many ways the most difficult if not the central problem of our free economy and our free society.

The current habit of dealing with the American economy in abstract statistical terms and in aggregates, averages, and dominant trends tempts us to forget or to slight the human scale, which must be the true measure by which economic activity in a democracy is to be judged. We have become somewhat accustomed in recent years to ever higher levels of unemployment to the point that such unemployment is sometimes described as normal. Weighing the statistics of unemployment against production and profits has moved some analysts to describe current unemployment as marginal in economic terms and marginal, therefore, in its claim upon our concern and our attention.

In each of the five years, 1958 and following, the rate of unemployment averaged 5½ percent or more, and unfortunately the rate in the United States has been relatively higher than in most other industrial countries. Moreover, the number of young workers in the labor force, which was about the same in 1960 as in 1950, will increase by 45 percent by 1970, a net addition of 6 million young workers in this decade. Also, dislocations caused by unemployment and technological change will increase.

Many thousands of Americans suffer long-term unemployment today because of age, race, lack of proper training, or obsolescence of once valued skills. Statistics alone cannot measure the human suffering caused by such persistent unemployment.

Let us look at specific industries or areas of employment. Agriculture, for example, has been greatly affected by both technical and nontechnological change. In 1860, workers in agriculture made up about 60 percent of the civilian labor force; in 1960 such workers made up less than 10 percent. There has been a definite decline not only in the relative number of persons engaged in agriculture, but in absolute numbers as well. In recent years there has been a significant shift out of agricultural employment—from 8.2 million in 1947 to 5.4 million in 1961—and with the improvements that have been and are being made in agricultural technology and methods, unemployment and underemployment among agricultural workers can be expected to increase. Further advances in this field will eliminate more workers, including a large percentage of the 2 million migrant workers. "Return of the masses to their normal and healthful existence as tillers of the soil," proposed in 1870 as a solution to unemployment in the cities, cannot be so considered today.

Employment in manufacturing relative to the size of our population has shown little change over the years. While the civilian population of the country increased by 61.7 percent between 1919 and 1956, employment in manufacturing industries increased by 60.5 percent. In absolute numbers, employment in manufacturing has increased much more slowly than has employment of nonproduction salaried workers.

In the electrical industry, according to the testimony of James B. Carey, president of the International Association of Electrical and Machine Workers, employment of production workers dropped from 925,000 in 1953 to 836,000 in February 1961, despite a large increase in the production of electrical appliances. According to Carey, also, instrument production, which has been expanding in recent years, now employs 30,000 fewer production workers than it did seven years ago—a drop of some 15 percent. In the manufacture of refrigerators and washing machines the decrease has been about 18 percent.

The testimony of Patrick E. Gorman, secretary-treasurer of the Amalgamated Meatcutters and Butcher Workers of North America, pointed out that although meat production increased in 1960, the total number of workers went down from 191,000 to 161,000. Despite increasing production, employment in this industry between 1956 and 1960 has been decreasing at a rate of more than 7,000 a year.

According to the testimony of David McDonald, president of the United Steelworkers of America, the year 1960 was almost identical with the year 1950 in terms of steel production and shipments. Yet in 1960 production-worker employ-

43

ment in steel averaged 461,800, compared with 540,000 in 1950—a decline of almost 80,000.

Mining has declined sharply as a source of employment. In 1919 mining accounted for 4.2 percent of all nonfarm employees; by 1947 it represented 2.2 percent of the non-farm employees, and in 1962 only 1.2 percent. The total number of men engaged in coal mining alone declined from nearly 500,000 in 1947 to 258,000 in 1955 and to an estimated 160,000 in 1962. The number employed in railroad transportation declined from 1,577,000 in 1947 to 1,205,000 in 1955 and to an estimated 801,000 in 1962. On the other hand, the number employed in truck transportation and storage increased from 551,000 in 1947 to 910,000 in 1962.

In the clerical field, automation has taken over the work of many clerks but, because of the increase in paper work, the number of people employed has tended to increase in spite of the machines.

In the retail trade there have been some changes: Introduction of vending machines has replaced a number of clerks, as is indicated by the volume of business done by these machines, which in 1960 totaled some $4 billion.

Solving the problem of unemployment, or approaching the solution to that problem, is not simply a matter of maintaining "prosperity." Since the end of World War II we have had "prosperity" in a relative sense, but in that period there have been three general economic recessions which have disrupted economic life and growth. Even when the economy has been operating at the top of the cycle, substantial areas of the country and numerous classes of our people have suffered some unemployment. We have not experienced mass unemployment of the Great Depression variety in recent years, but large numbers of people have been affected by class unemployment.

When unemployment is widespread because of a sweeping cyclical change in the whole economy, there is general awareness of its existence and of its consequences. But chronic local unemployment remains out of sight because statistically it does not involve a high percentage of the national labor force or many areas of the country. The wide community of the nation forgets or overlooks the fact that some cities and areas of our country are chronically ill, and that only the crudest home remedies are being applied to what are grave economic problems.

What is the conservative answer? One argument is that a certain amount of unemployment is necessary to lubricate the economic machine; that there must always be workers

44

changing jobs, industries declining as others rise, and a ready labor supply available for new products or extra shifts.

A second conservative argument is that current unemployment is temporary.

A third conservative argument is that the problem is local, that it should be left to industry or to the states.

A fourth is, of course, the easy and necessary recommendation of increase in the rate of national economic growth and a higher level of economic activity for the country.

It must be accepted that there will be some unemployment in a complex and changing economy, but it does not follow that unemployment should entail hardship, or that it should be prolonged, or that we should make no effort to keep it to a minimum.

Unfortunately, theories are too often used to explain away unemployment as a necessary evil or even a positive good. If this economic argument has validity, we should be much more generous in our financial provisions for the jobless, since even in their unemployment they make a positive contribution to the economy. The people who are idle because they cannot meet an employer's entrance requirements, or because they are not suitably located, perform only a minor labor-supply function in our economy. And chronic unemployment, which has crippled and is still crippling scores of American communities, contributes nothing whatever to our economy.

Economic theories should not divert us from the simple, positive response that justice demands when we see the misery and hopelessness in which too many of our people now live. Evasion of their just claim for help is faulty democracy as well as bad economics.

The fact is that unemployment is a serious and continuing problem. The indications are that it will assume far greater importance in the next ten years unless decisive action is taken. After each of the last three recessions, the rate of unemployment was higher than it had been before the recession began.

The problem of unemployment is a national problem in part because it results from complex forces, most of which are national in origin or in nature. Every section of the country suffers the effects of unemployment and of decreased purchasing power. Local communities with the highest rates of unemployment are often those with the fewest tax and economic resources. Many local communities, despite extraordinary efforts, have been unable to create sufficient jobs.

The liberal position emphasizes federal responsibility. The

Congress expressed this positive approach in the Employment Act of 1946, the preamble of which states:

"The Congress declares that it is the continuing policy and responsibility of the Federal Government to use all practicable means consistent with its needs and obligations and other essential considerations of national policy, with the assistance and cooperation of industry, agriculture, labor, and State and local governments, to coordinate and utilize all its plans, functions, and resources for the purpose of creating and maintaining, in a manner calculated to foster and promote free competitive enterprise and the general welfare, conditions under which there will be afforded useful employment opportunities, including self-employment, for those able, willing, and seeking to work, and to promote maximum employment, production, and purchasing power."

Private and public measures must be taken to absorb the people who are currently unemployed and are certainly necessary to provide employment for the 26 million young people who will enter the labor force in the decade 1960–70.

In addition there is a need for special assistance in distressed areas: to revitalize industry where this is possible, to establish new industries where it is economically feasible, to facilitate the movement of people to new areas of employment when revitalization is impossible. Beginnings have been made in the Area Redevelopment Act of 1961, although it is of limited scope and effectiveness.

There is a need for the establishment of national standards for federal-state systems of unemployment insurance to extend coverage and provide adjustments in weeks of protection and amount of benefits, as well as in financing the systems.

The structure of unemployment has changed to a point where restrictions on coverage based on size of firm and type of employment should be removed, at least so far as the basic unemployment compensation is concerned—that is, that element of unemployment which can be attributed to national trends and national forces. Benefit formulas, too, should be changed to extend the length of time during which benefits will be paid since, again on the basis of the record, it is evident that unemployment is lasting for longer and longer periods. The changing over to modern and automated equipment takes longer than it formerly took to retool in simpler industrial operations. The movement of industry from one part of the country to another also complicates the problems of adjustment and changes the time schedule.

The benefits generally paid in the states have been too low to provide reasonable support for the unemployed person and his family. These benefits should be raised to roughly 50 percent, at least, of regular weekly earnings.

Those industries which have special problems of unemployment should be required to make corresponding contributions to unemployment insurance which, of course, would be reflected in the prices charged for goods and services.

Also, the federal government should stand ready with emergency public works programs to help meet the very special problems of recessions or unusual temporary disturbances in the economic life of the country.

In some industries attempts have been made to work out the adjustments that result from automation, increased productivity, or displacement of men by machines. In the case of the coal mining industry and the United Mine Workers under John L. Lewis, special funds were established to help to relieve distress and the pressure of transition in a period of automation, increased use of other fuels, and changes in user practices. In the railroad industry similar practices have been followed.

On a broader scale, improved unemployment compensation programs, supported out of general revenue or by employers, have been proposed. According to one proposal, these programs would be supported by a special tax placed upon machines. As a machine displaced a man and became more productive, a portion of the increased productivity would be drawn off in the way of taxes. This tax in turn would be used to establish a fund which would meet the special problems of readjustment or existence of the displaced worker.

None of these approaches meets the problem of providing employment for young people or new people coming into the working force, or for those who may wish to change from one type of employment to another. Proposals have been made for a shorter working day, a shorter working week, a shorter working year, or a shorter working lifetime—earlier retirement, longer vacations. In 1900 the six-day, 60-hour week was about average, while today, aside from agriculture, the eight-hour day and five-day week are standard.

All of these proposals are deserving of some consideration, and are receiving some. A program of retraining has been advocated, and the Manpower Development and Train-

47

ing Act approved by Congress in 1962 provides for such a program. There is, of course, a need for retraining, but the possibility of its solving the total problem is extremely remote.

The distressed area redevelopment legislation that has been approved is basically distressed industry legislation. Proposals have been submitted and provisions made for a geographical shift to try to help the surplus working force move from one area of the country to another where job opportunities are greater. But these proposals have been somewhat limited, and have been subject to negotiation by labor unions. It has been suggested that tax deduction, at least, be given for the costs incurred by a worker in moving himself and his family from one part of the country to another in order to obtain work.

Each of these proposals has in it some potentiality for good. Some of them can be made effective through government action; most of them, certainly, can be assisted by government. Others can be advanced either primarily by negotiation between labor and management or by unilateral action on the part of management. In each case there is a need for public understanding and some measure of public response.

In a liberal view, "the right to work" is too closely related to basic human rights to be used as a mere slogan against unionization.

For most citizens the opportunity to work means, of course, the opportunity to make a livelihood; but work is more than an economic activity. The full consideration of unemployment must take into account the nature of work and its meaning to the human being. Neither unrelieved leisure activities nor idleness is the road to happiness. Man by nature needs more than satisfaction of his capacity to consume. He needs also to produce, to construct, to add some degree of perfection to goods or to provide services for other men.

☆☆☆ *Chapter 3*

THE CHALLENGE OF AUTOMATION

Meeting the simple material needs of man is not the answer to all of his problems. There are other forms of poverty. New challenges arise daily. A recently published book by

Henry Brandon, entitled *As We Are,* contains conversations with a number of learned and thoughtful people. These conversations bear on the poverty of ideas and of creative thought in our social and political structure.

In one of these conversations, the anthropologist Margaret Mead observes: "None of us know how to run cities. We don't know how to run large aggregations of people. We don't know how to make the average citizen in a country of this size take responsibility. We don't know it here, and they don't know it in the Soviet Union. The Soviet Union uses the secret police and every form of suppression, because they are afraid of ignorance and misdirected energies of the mass of the people. The methods that we use here are not so much methods as lack of methods, in which we let delinquency and crime and alcoholism and political corruption build up and corrode our capacities to behave as a people."

In another conversation, Professor Norbert Wiener replies as follows to a question about whether American society has begun to struggle against the machines: "No, because the advances made by the machines are likely to come so rapidly that unless the adjustment is a little bit in advance of that —the adjustment to the way of thought—we're likely to be left high and dry. One of the surprising things with modern technique is that every apparatus, every method is obsolete by the time it is used. Techniques are developing so rapidly that we cannot, unless we are going to have a large period of chaos, allow our thinking to lag behind the techniques and the possible modes of development."

In reply to an observation that automation causes an atrophy in the creative desires of man, he said:

> "That *is* very serious. I mean, when you degrade the skilled worker to a machine hand, you are not only making a change in efficiency for the particular job, but you can to a considerable extent destroy him as a human being; this is just the sort of thing I'm talking about. . . .
>
> "I would give the advice that society at large and government should be sufficiently informed about its own social purposes to be able to use these new tools for the certain consideration of these purposes instead of as purely technical devices where the whole ideal is massive production. I think that the factory system, as we know it, is taken by many of us today too much for granted, as belonging to society in general instead of to a very recent period of history, and that in judging automatiza-

49

tion we are combining it with the state after the First Industrial Revolution rather than finding how we can act in society in general and interpreting society sufficiently deeply to make the proper use of it. In other words, the combination of the 19th century factory system with automation—I think is devastating. We cannot ignore social effects like that with respect to pure economic effects and expect to avoid chaos."

Moral judgment concerning automation should take into account two things: first, the nature of work and the effect of automation upon man as a worker; and second, the consequences in terms of social, economic, and cultural change that may result from automation. If work in itself were a curse, then a fully automated productive system would be wholly desirable—a kind of temporal redemption. On the other hand, if work is considered as a merited temporal punishment, elimination of labor is a most dangerous venture.

The case both for and against automation is unclear. There are those who say that with it there will be demands for greater skill and greater intellectual response, and that work will then be truly more creative and much drudgery will be eliminated. There are others who say that automated work will become increasingly uncreative and that, whereas this work may not be drudgery according to the traditional or classical definition, it will involve a kind of intellectual drudgery, depressing the mind, and discouraging, if not eliminating, the need for the exercise of creative talents and capacity.

Work is an activity which for most men is an expression of the human person. If it is established that automation dehumanizes the worker, then we must pass a moral judgment upon it, since work which is becoming to man should allow the use of intelligence and the exercise of moral responsibility and of creative talent.

There are those who say that with the advance of automation there will be a need for more advanced technicians, more supervisors, more managers, that we will need more people and a higher percentage of the working force who are better trained and better skilled as technicians, as engineers, and the like.

There are others who say that this result will not necessarily follow and that, in fact, fewer skilled people will be needed; that workers will not have to have the same degree of mastery of technique and of knowledge that they now need; that many will be displaced or demoted from semiskilled and semiprofessional positions they now hold to positions requiring less skill and intelligence and more limited application.

There are some who say that the effect of today's automation is different from the effect of early mechanization and the development of the factory system, because in earlier times when people were displaced they could move down to take jobs which required somewhat less skill or they might move up to more skilled positions; now, they say, there is little room at the top and little room at the bottom, since automation is removing not only the semiskilled jobs but also those which require the least skill.

If this is the case, and if unemployment, consequently, becomes a more serious and permanent problem, the moral responsibility of society to attempt to ease and to overcome these effects is clear. If automation is to eliminate jobs at the middle, then certainly we must undertake to make more room at the top by training more people for professions and skilled occupations, and make at least enough room at the bottom so that the less skilled or less gifted can earn a living with some decency and certainty.

There are some who say that with automation there will be fewer jobs for women; others say it will increase the demand. Some experts say that, because of the greater investment in capital, the practice of employing swing shifts and even night shifts will increase. If the practice of running factories 24 hours a day does increase, if it becomes widespread, this development certainly will have significant implications with regard to family life and to the whole structure of society.

Without trying to form a final judgment as to how bad things may become as automation progresses or how good they may be, one can fairly assume that there will be problems in the future, some of which will be caused by automation. Accepting that there will be problems, we must ask two questions: One, can anything be done, or should it be done; and two, assuming that something can and should be done, how and by whom.

Since automation involves principally the industrial and business world, immediate responsibility rests upon those who are most directly involved. Those who lead organized labor, as well as unorganized labor, share the burden of responsibility with management and the directors of industry. In addition, everyone who in any way participates either as a producer or a consumer in our economy must accept some measure of responsibility. The responsibility of

51

the latter is most likely to be expressed through some form of governmental activity.

Long before the 19th century when the problems of mechanization and of the factory system became matters of general concern, Queen Elizabeth denied a patent for a knitting machine sought by one Mr. William Lee because, she is quoted as having said, "I have too much regard for my people who obtain their bread by knitting."

In the middle of the 19th century, John Stuart Mill, writing as a philosopher of liberal economics, said that there cannot be a more "legitimate object of the legislator's care than the interests of those who are thus sacrificed to the gain of their fellow citizens and posterity—those displaced by changing methods of production."

There are still other ways in which this whole problem of welfare can be considered in a somewhat broader context of ideas and institutions. We need to give some thought to the basic concept of ownership in our society and in our economy. It is generally recognized now that for most people in the United States, ownership is not what it was a hundred years ago. Generally the great body of productive property is not tangible, identifiable real property, but exists in claims to income.

This is certainly true in the case of the claims of the corporate stockholder, and of those who hold bonds, insurance policies, and so forth. Most workers do not own the tools with which they work, but lay claim to a job and to a salary or wages which they are to receive for performing their work. The question of ownership is involved not in an absolute but in a relative sense in such issues as that of the closed shop or the right of a person to hold a job.

In hearings before the Congress several years ago, this point was dramatized by a comparison of arguments being made before two separate committees. One was the Interior Committee, which was proposing to change the lease arrangements on public lands being used for cattle grazing. The request was for a change in the terms of the leases so as to give the individuals holding them modified and greatly strengthened rights of use and of transfer.

A witness in favor of the legislation supported the proposition with two arguments: That those who already held the leases should be given the new leases, first, because of "priority"—that is, because they were already there—and, second, because of "stability"—the witness argued that to put the leases up at auction might have the effect of disturbing the whole community.

52

At the same time hearings were being held before the Labor Committee on the question of the closed shop. Spokesmen for the same group that argued for property rights based upon priority and stability in the case of public land leases opposed the closed shop, while spokesmen for organized labor argued that the worker's right to the job should be recognized for two reasons: one, "priority," because the worker was already there; and two, for reasons of the "stability" of society. In each case the traditional or original—sometimes called natural—claims to ownership, occupancy, priority, and stability, were being advanced to cover new circumstances.

There have been two rather significant federal court decisions touching upon the vested rights of employees. When Gemmer, a Detroit unit of the Ross Gear and Tool Manufacturing Company of Indiana, decided to move to Lebanon, Tennessee, and declined to offer transfers to the main body of its United Auto Workers employees, a bargaining committee of the Auto Workers sued on behalf of the employees. The judge sustained the contention of the union, holding that the rights claimed by the employees extend "beyond the time limitations of the collective bargaining agreement." They apply, he said, to the company plant "regardless of physical location under this and previous contracts." He held that the company "has the obligation and duty to rehire on the basis of seniority" employees laid off in Detroit, even though the move to Lebanon might terminate the role of their union as their bargaining agent.

This 1961 ruling expanded an earlier decision by the Second Circuit Court of Appeals in what is known as the Glidden case. In this case the court held, in 1957, that employees had acquired by their continuous service "vested rights" that the company could not unilaterally deny.

Throughout the years many of the larger corporations have developed a structure in which, through various devices, employees increasingly are tied to the company. Pension programs, medical and health insurance, special unemployment compensation, supplemental unemployment benefits, profit sharing, job rights, and a number of other benefits, either real or prospective, create bonds between the employee and the company for which he works. Many of these programs have been sought by organized labor.

Another extreme manifestation of this was reflected several years ago in a *Fortune* magazine series entitled "The Wives of Management," in which the concern of the corporation extended not only to the life of its employee while on the job, but to the social structure of which he was a part. It was suggested by one corporate director that the

53

corporation should not wait until after marriage, but ought to be concerned about giving some direction and guidance to its employees in the *selection* of wives. Possibilities of this kind of direct and indirect control are practically unlimited, especially now that calculators, computers, and mechanical brains have been perfected to do the sorting.

The choice may be to fix more and more responsibility upon corporations to accept the fact that their employees are their charges and to insist that the employees receive in return for their work a fair share from the production of the particular industry. This share could be defined so as to include not only immediate wages, but all those things which are now commonly lumped under the title of "fringe benefits."

On the other hand the decision may be to establish or maintain national programs of security: to improve the social security program so as to make it more effective, to have a national program of health insurance, to have a more satisfactory unemployment compensation program based upon national standards. The decision need not be absolute on one side or the other, but certainly there is a need for consideration of the possibility that the corporate plans may very well have the effect of limiting the economic and social mobility as well as the general freedom of individual employees. Therefore this individual freedom may need to be somewhat secured by national programs which establish a reasonable base, leaving to the individual a measure of freedom and a greater measure of choice. This problem exists not only for the working man, but for professional and semiprofessional people as well.

An improved, reasonably adequate national retirement program would make it easier for an employee who wanted to leave a particular job. It would at least put him in a position so that if he wanted to leave he would not be under pressure to stay because of his company pension program; rather, he could choose to leave and still carry with him some measure of security against old age.

Or if there were a national program of health insurance, a person who might wish to leave would not be held to his original job because he could not afford to give up his medical insurance program. Or if a reasonably effective national unemployment compensation program were in effect, a person who wished to leave the employ of one company or one industry to go to another would not be bound to stay with the first one on the grounds that if he were to leave he would lose all the benefits and rights he had accumulated in that job. This would provide flexibility similar to that now guaranteed for old age retirement benefits under the Social Security Act.

Are we moving toward a point where a difficult choice may have to be made between a kind of corporate feudalism and a broader and more personal economic and social structure?

One charge against capitalism and the free enterprise system made by the Marxists is that whereas the capitalistic system is able to produce in great quantities, it does not have within itself the potential for working out the problem of distribution. Certainly this problem is a complicated and difficult one. But the more serious problem developing now is not that of the distribution of production, but rather the distribution of participation in productive effort and productive work. This is a more fundamental consideration. We have been challenged to work out devices and procedures under which every person can have a claim and a share in the productive effort of our economy and, on the basis of that participation, a claim to a share of that which is produced. Neither New Deal nor pre-New Deal thought gives a ready answer to these difficult problems. Neither traditional conservative appeals for a free market economy and for competition, nor traditional liberal appeals for simple extension or interpretation of New Deal programs or ideas, is adequate.

Part III

The Responsibilities of Responsible Government

☆☆☆ *Chapter 1*
UPS AND DOWNS ON THE FARM

The Jeffersonian idea of political democracy assumed the existence of an agrarian society made up basically of independent farm owners. This idea was reflected during and immediately following the Revolutionary War when action was taken to abolish entail (the system under which inalienable hereditary estates were preserved) and when large estates were broken up.

It was reflected, too, in a series of legislative actions taken by the national Congress soon after the adoption of the Constitution. These acts made frontier lands available to individual farmers in small acreage and at low cost. Later, in the Homestead Act of 1862 and other similar legislation, land was given at no cost to settlers who met minimum conditions. During the next century, approximately 1½ million Americans acquired some 250 million acres of free land.

America was primarily rural in population until the census of 1920, which was the first to show that the urban population was larger than the rural, and by 1961 the nation was 70 percent urban. The farm population declined from nearly 32 million in 1920 to about 15.6 million in 1962. In 1920 the farm population made up 30 percent of the population; in 1962 it made up less than 9 percent. In the 30-year period since 1930 the number of farms decreased from 6.5 million to fewer than 4 million.

While these numerical changes have been taking place and while there have been shifts in the social structure of the United States, there have also been significant economic changes in American agriculture. There are many ways to measure the great achievements of agriculture. Some of them are worth reviewing before we examine the problems and explore possible solutions.

The average American farmer today produces enough to feed and clothe 27 people. In Europe an average farmer produces enough for about ten people. In Russia, under a collective system, the farmer produces enough for only four or five. In many nations of the world most people live on the land because it is the only way they can get enough food to eat.

The efficiency of the American farmer has helped keep the cost of food to consumers at relatively low levels. In this country the average family spends about 20 percent of its income for food. In Great Britain, food takes over 30 percent of the family income; in Italy, 45 percent. In Russia the average family spends over 60 percent of its income for food. In many parts of the world food costs take 70 to 80 percent of the worker's earnings.

One farmer in 1962 produced as much as four did in 1910. The agricultural output per man-hour doubled between 1950 and 1961, and in recent years the American farmer has surpassed the industrial worker in productive efficiency. Between 1950 and 1960 the output of the average farm worker increased at an annual rate of 6.5 percent, or three times as fast as the productivity of the man in the factory.

The United States is by far the world's largest exporter of agricultural products and supplies about one-fifth of all farm products moving in world trade. It is estimated that in 1960 the output of 60 million acres of our cropland, or about one in every six harvested, went into exports to foreign consumers. In fiscal year 1962 we shipped farm commodities valued at $5 billion, a new record. This includes donations and sales for local currencies under the Agricultural Trade Development and Assistance Act (popularly known as Public Law 480) as well as subsidized exports for dollars. Together these government-financed operations account for approximately 60 percent of our exports.

Almost three billion pounds of food was distributed to over 100 nations through voluntary relief agencies and intergovernmental organizations. People everywhere have benefited because of the efficiency and productivity of the American farmer. Many people throughout the world are impressed by our industrial accomplishments and our military strength; many more are impressed by the fact that fewer than 9 percent of our people can produce more food than our nation can consume.

Despite this great record of production, there is in the United States what is called a "farm problem," and many agricultural areas of this country are depressed. Of course, American farm families do not live in the abject poverty of the landless peasantry of many parts of the world, but real poverty does exist in many rural areas.

More than one-half of our farm families are in the lowest one-fifth of the nation's income groups. Incomes of farm families are lower relative to the rest of the population than they have been at any time since the depression of the 1930's. The hourly return for labor on farms in 1960 was less than 82 cents, compared to $2.29 for factory workers. Average annual income per capita for people on farms was $986 (of which $329 came from nonfarm sources), compared to $2,282 per capita for the nonfarm population.

The decline in farm population reflects the economic plight of the farmer. The efficient family farmer has found it necessary to increase his acreage to make full use of machine-based technologies. He has bought or rented land from the small farmer who lacked resources to use the new technology. It is estimated that 220,000 farm boys reach working age each year, but there are only 23,000 openings for new people on farms promising an annual net income of $1,500 for the farm family. Ninety percent of the young male workers in farm families must look to nonagricultural pursuits, or accept the lowest levels of farm income. Many small farmers have given up or turned to whatever non-farm work they could find in order to remain in rural communities.

Distress in the agricultural economy is not new; for most of the past 40 years there has been difficulty. Agriculture was depressed during the Twenties and of course the economic condition became worse during the general depression of the Thirties. In the decade since the Korean conflict, the farm problem has again become a public question of first magnitude.

The problem is many-faceted, reflecting at once the economic disorder resulting from surplus production and the social disorder resulting from poverty and from the displacement of people. There are international as well as national implications to the problem. It is complicated by expanding production in Canada, Western Europe, Australia, New Zealand, and some of the countries of South America. With most of these countries unable or unwilling to accept greater amounts of surplus agricultural supplies from other countries, the agricultural depression deepens and spreads at the expense of both "have" and "have-not" nations.

The disparity between public services available to farm and nonfarm people is relatively as great in the United States as in other nations of the world. Health and educational deficiencies are especially marked, but these are no less serious than deficiencies in housing, transportation, and communication in many areas.

Improvement of those services which are a public responsibility cannot await the ultimate solution of the economic problem. They are a part of it, and must be accorded proper attention within any balanced and comprehensive attack on the sources of the present agricultural crisis.

The fact is that there is no one farm problem. There are many problems of varying degrees and importance and intensity, some of them arising from within the agricultural economy and some of them impinging on it from outside. The problem involves not only economic considerations, but social and political ones as well.

In the United States there is a relatively clear division between what we call the liberal approach to these problems and the conservative approach. For the most part, the conservatives, with little regard for history, argue that the answer to the farm problem rests in the elimination or discontinuation of government programs and in the operation of a free market for agricultural commodities—at least, they would say, within the domestic economy. It is clear to all that such proposals cannot be made in international trade because of the unwillingness of most of the other countries of the world to accept free international trade in agricultural products.

In fact, the conservatives set some limitations upon their advocacy of free exchange even within the domestic economy of the United States. For the most part they accept some existing programs dealing with specific commodities, such as the programs established by the Sugar Act and the Wool Act, and generally they are not for the elimination of all price supports, although they usually argue for a lower base and for greater flexibility.

The liberal position, on the other hand, has been one in which somewhat more far-reaching participation on the part of government has been advocated. There is general agreement as to objectives. The disagreement comes over method and over the question of the role of government in the total picture.

Some progress has been made during recent sessions of Congress.

In 1962 the net farm income of $12.9 billion was 10 percent higher than in 1960 and the highest since 1953. Farm exports rose to a record high of $5.1 billion. Average income per farm was up 13 percent, from $2,960 to $3,360. Hourly return per farm worker was 99 cents, compared with 82 cents in 1960. Bank deposits and business activity in 20 major farm states increased by 10 percent above 1960.

The 1961 and 1962 voluntary feed grain programs reduced carry-over stocks of feed grains and Commodity Credit Corporation investment in them, and reduced government costs for storage and handling of unneeded production.

Each year since 1950 production of feed grains had outstripped use and surpluses had increased. The carry-over of feed grains increased from 28.6 million tons in 1950 to 84.7 million tons at the beginning of the 1961 marketing year.

The Commodity Credit Corporation investment in feed grains had increased from $1.1 billion in 1950 to $3.4 billion in September 1961. The feed grain programs reversed this rising trend. Most of the reduction in stocks since 1961 has been in those owned or controlled by the government.

Total feed grain stocks in 1961 were reduced by 12.9 million tons. The Department of Agriculture estimates that if the voluntary feed grain program had not been in effect, stocks would have increased by approximately 6.8 million tons, a net difference of 19.7 tons. For 1962 they estimated that the net difference in stocks would amount to approximately 23.2 million tons; for 1963, about 18.2 million tons.

The Department estimated that the ultimate net savings due to the operation of the feed grain programs, after deducting all costs, and including acreage diversion payments, will be about as follows:

1961 program	$ 591 million
1962 program	634 million
1963 program	143 million
Total	$1,368 million

These ultimate savings are based on acquisitions avoided as follows:

1961	704 million bushels
1962	820 million bushels
1963	625 million bushels
Total	2,149 million bushels

Producers voluntarily retired around 25 million acres

from production under the 1961 program and nearly 29 million acres under the 1962 program. Diversion payments to farmers totaled $782 million in 1961, $842 million in 1962, and an estimated $472 million in 1963.

On the whole, the actions of recent Congresses represent a constructive response to the immediate problems of agriculture. They continue programs highly important to the welfare of the farm family and make some significant improvements. Taken together, these actions promise to improve farm income and reduce government costs and government-held surpluses.

Government price support programs have been developed to meet the problems related to a particular commodity rather than as an across-the-board subsidy for farmers. Programs have been added and dropped. Sometimes adjustments have been required. The dairy program worked reasonably well for several years, but the dairy situation became serious in 1962. Government costs to maintain dairy prices had averaged less than $300 million annually from 1949 through 1960, but then reached nearly $600 million in fiscal year 1962. In that year the Commodity Credit Corporation acquired 9 percent of the butter fat and 13 percent of the nonfat solids of all the milk marketed by the farmers of the nation. Even though price supports under the law dropped from 82 to 75 percent of parity, estimates of government costs for the program in 1963 were in excess of $500 million.

One of the chief causes of the dairy problem was the significant decline in milk consumption in 1961. Milk production increased by 1.5 percent, while milk consumption declined by 2.5 percent. This decline occurred despite an increase in population and a significant expansion of the school lunch and special school milk programs.

Americans used more than 100 billion pounds of dairy foods in 1961, but this was still over 2 billion pounds less than they had used the previous year.

In the situation facing the dairy industry, increased consumption—especially of fluid milk—would obviously be the most desirable of the possible remedies. Americans should be drinking more milk, which remains one of the best of all foods nutritionally and one of the least expensive. We are told that most people are drinking less milk than the amount recommended for good health. Although no one can determine the exact reasons for the decline in the use of milk products, it does present economic problems in managing and marketing milk production. And what may be even more serious in the long run, it endangers the balanced use

61

of soil, water and animal resources which has always made dairying a mainstay of sound conservation practices.

For the immediate future, it is increasingly clear that farmers must choose between efforts to adjust production and stabilize prices or the abandonment of all farm programs, with the resulting decline in income which history indicates will inevitably follow.

Farmers cannot turn back to the myths of the past, nor can we cling to halfway answers. In a sense, at this point in history farmers are again called upon to pioneer. The farmer has always pioneered—he opened the West and settled the land; he was responsible for the initial efforts to establish the land grant college system for the dissemination of scientific and technical information. Also, he pioneered in economic organizations, through such devices as the co-operative as a means of better marketing. He pioneered in political organizations in an attempt to obtain economic justice. And he has pioneered in legislative remedies designed to enable a nation to make the most of its abundance.

Farmers, with the support of government programs, can adjust their production to the needs of domestic and foreign markets and achieve fair price levels and a fair return for their effort. This course offers the only real freedom of action, of individual management decision, to the American farmer. It is not a new or revolutionary procedure in the economic life of the country. It has been tested in industry and in some segments of agriculture. It offers new possibilities for meeting the challenges of change in the complicated world of the 1960's. Our problems are different and vastly more complex than they were 100 years ago, but responsible men are capable of devising intelligent responses to these problems.

The basic objectives of the farm program must be: to raise average farm incomes and to stabilize them; to increase agricultural efficiency for the benefit of all society; and to work out effective methods of distribution. These objectives often conflict.

To check the movement out of agriculture, immediate steps are necessary to permit rural families to share more fully in the advances made in housing, transportation, communication, health care, educational opportunities, and recreational facilities. These are not ends in themselves but means for the development of a well-ordered community life in which man can fulfill his nature in dignity.

☆☆☆ *Chapter 2*
HEALTH FOR THE ELDERLY

In a special message to the Congress on November 19, 1945, President Truman requested the enactment of a national health program. His message was stated in rather broad and general terms. He recommended the broadest possible coverage for all who work for a living and for their dependents, and also recomemnded that the needy be covered through the public assistance program. The amount of benefits was not specified; the general recommendation was that provision should be made for payment to doctors, to hospitals, to dentists, and to nurses.

He suggested a decentralized administration for the health program—one that could be based upon a local administrative unit, so that services could be provided and adapted to local needs and conditions—and suggested that the program be financed through an increase in the social security levy and by appropriation of additional funds from the general revenue. Mr. Truman repeated his call for a national health program in 1947 and again in 1949.

In 1961 and again in 1963, President Kennedy made recommendations for a program restricted to the hospital and nursing home needs of the aged in our population.

Almost every conceivable argument has been made in opposition to these medical and hospital aid programs: The professional one, that they would interfere with the practice of medicine; the economic one, that they would place too great a burden upon the economy of the country; the practical one, that the program is unnecessary; and the procedural one, that the objective is good but that the methods, procedures, and program being recommended are highly unsatisfactory. There are also some rather curious arguments such as that made by those who say that the plan is all right for a starter, but that it goes too far; or on the other hand, that it is a very dangerous precedent or beginning, but that the coverage is not extensive enough.

The first question to be asked is whether there is any need for a hospital aid program for persons over 65. Certainly the medical needs and problems of the aged fall into a separate class and, therefore, deserve special attention. One out of six of the aged is hospitalized every year, and once admitted to a hospital his average stay is two weeks (twice as long as the average stay for younger patients). It is estimated that, of those over 65, nine out of ten will be hospitalized at least once before they die. The record shows that persons over 65 are twice as likely as younger people to suffer chronic conditions of ill health.

It is true that financial responsibilities of the aged are not as great as those of younger people. They do not have the expenses of starting out in the professions or in business or of paying for a home, nor are they pressed to provide for the care and education of their children. But if their responsibilities are reduced, so is their income. Fewer than one in four people in the United States over age 65 have any income from employment; the great majority live on savings, social security benefits, public assistance payments, contributions from their children, or similar sources of income.

The majority of those over 65 today have a very limited income. In 1960 the median money income of men over 65 was about $1,600, and 45 percent of them had incomes of less than $1,500 a year. In 1960 only 6.3 percent of all persons over 65 had money incomes of $5,000 or more. Only a half million of the aged lived in institutions in 1961; seven out of ten lived alone or with their spouse or another relative.

The great majority of the aged have been able to meet ordinary expenses. But if anyone suffers prolonged illness, hospital and medical costs can quickly use all his savings and may even result in his leaving an inheritance of debt incurred because of the illness. For many older persons, the great unknown and uncertain economic factor in their lives is the prospect of sickness, in the face of a growing incapacity to take care of themselves and inability to meet the expenses of prolonged illness—a prospect which Shakespeare described in *As You Like It* as the last age of man:

> "The last scene of all,
> That ends this strange eventful history,
> Is second childishness, and mere oblivion,
> Sans teeth, sans eyes, sans taste, sans everything."

Some opponents of legislation in this area seem to accept this gloomy picture as necessary and inevitable.

If the need is acknowledged, the next question is whether the establishment of an insurance system or of some other system for assisting the aged to meet their special medical or hospital needs is a responsibility of government. Many conservatives say that it is not.

In a column entitled "Medical Care for the Aged" in the *Washington Post* for June 16, 1960, Walter Lippmann asked: "Why does the President [Eisenhower] feel so strongly opposed to the principle of compulsory insurance for medical care to supplement the insurance which already exists for old age? What is wrong about its being compulsory that a man should insure himself against the needs of his old age? What is so wonderful about a voluntary system under which a man who doesn't save for his old age has to have his doctors and his hospital bills paid for by his children or public welfare funds?" He noted that, "Among the opponents of medical insurance there seems to be a vague and uncomfortable feeling that it is a new-fangled theory, alien to the American way of life and imported, presumably, from Soviet Russia."

Much of what is said in this vein is similar to what was said about the social security retirement program when it was first proposed. It was labeled foreign and socialistic. It was said to be contrary to traditional American values, and was branded a threat to the whole structure of our society.

So today we are told that a federal program would constitute socialized medicine but that a mixed state-federal program, or a purely state program, would not. I have never seen a definition of socialism which would establish the distinction that what is done by the federal government is socialistic but that what is done by state government or by the state and federal governments acting together somehow becomes unsocialistic.

In either case the program is a governmental one; the laws are enacted by legislatures, either state or federal. The distinction, then, is not one of socialism as opposed to some other form of political or economic ideology, but rather one of practical means and procedures. It has been argued that once the federal government moves to meet a particular problem, complete federal control or operation inevitably follows. The overwhelming weight of evidence in our national history is against this assertion.

If this argument had prevailed in the past, we would be a strange nation today. To be consistent, those who make this argument should be advocating a return to the Articles of Confederation. There were prophets in 1787 who said that a federal union would destroy the identity and the authority of the states and make them completely subject to an all-powerful central government; the refrain is an old one.

In actual fact, the states have continued to exercise initiative and to play a paramount role in many areas: in education, in matters relating to the protection of public health and safety and morals, and in many new areas of decision required by changes in the economic and social structure of America.

There are those who argue that private insurance, together with state aid for the indigent sick, is adequate. The obvious answer is that for many this has not been the case. Private companies are doing an important job in the field of health insurance. However, the private insurance companies' inability to meet the total problem is a matter of simple economics: Most of the aged cannot be adequately insured on an individual basis. The fact that private policies return on the average only 50 percent of the premiums collected results in such high costs that very few of the aged in need of medical care can afford to pay for adequate protection on this basis.

The government might subsidize the private insurance companies—there is no real argument against this 'n principle, if it is the best and most economical way to accomplish the purpose. The same argument, however, could be applied to social security, and experience has shown that this program, including nearly all citizens of the United States, has been most effective as a national program.

Nearly all of the existing state programs have an individual income limit of $1,200 to $1,500 annually, beyond which point the individual becomes ineligible for medical aid. About half of the state programs provide no assistance where the yearly income exceeds $2,000 per couple. More than half of the states deny benefits to individuals whose liquid assets exceed $1,000. In half of the states, couples with liquid assets of more than $1,300 are ineligible.

The range of benefits varies from emergency care, in states like Kentucky and Tennessee, to comprehensive care in states like Massachusetts and New York. State requirements with regard to the responsibility of relatives vary greatly: Some provide for a determination of the ability of adult children to assume the financial burden; some attempt to use the device of a statutory formula based upon the income of listed relatives.

As early as 1946, Senator Taft recognized the need for a better program. His recommendation then was for a system of federal grants to the states for planning and carrying out programs to provide medical and other health services to medically needy persons. He included in his program families and individuals unable to pay the whole cost of needed medical and hospital services; he also included dental services, with limitations. His proposal was substantially the same as that which has now been adopted in the Kerr-Mills law, with federal grants made to the states on a variable matching basis, depending on the per capita income of the people of the state.

In the 87th Congress, the Kennedy Administration's hospital insurance program for the aged was introduced in the Senate by Senator Anderson of New Mexico, and in the House by Representative King of California. Basically, it proposed health benefits for people over 65 who were eligible for Old Age and Survivors' Insurance benefits or railroad retirement annuities. Altogether, slightly over 14 million persons would have been eligible.

The benefits or payments would have been made for the following kinds of services: in-patient hospital care, skilled nursing home care after transfer from hospitals, home health services, and out-patient diagnostic services. There were limitations on all of these services and limitations, too, as to the number of days during which hospital or nursing home care might be provided.

It was estimated that the total cost of providing these benefits would be slightly over $1 billion a year in the beginning, increasing to about $2 billion a year in the long run. These costs were to be met by raising from $4,800 to $5,200 the amount of annual earnings subject to social security payroll tax and by increasing the tax rate by one-half of one percent of taxable earnings beginning in 1963—one-fourth of one percent to be paid by the employer and a matching amount to be paid by the employee. In the case of the self-employed, there was to be a total increase of .375 percent. Payments were to be made to the hospital or clinic or to the vendor, with no dictation as to choice of doctor or hospital, provided only that they be properly accredited.

In response to criticism, supporters of the bill later agreed to extend coverage to include all persons over 65, with the federal government providing payments out of general revenue for those not covered by social security.

The Anderson bill provided an option under which beneficiaries could receive health benefits from private insurance, through group practice or other voluntary nongovernmental programs, and it contained explicit provisions to insure that the federal government would not interfere in the practice of medicine or the operation of medical institutions. For example, it provided that hospitals accredited by the Joint Commission on the Accreditation of Hospitals would be conclusively presumed to meet all the statutory requirements for participation.

This is more protection than is provided in the Kerr-Mills Act, which grants the state welfare director broad power to determine administrative policies, with the provision that the state plans have to be federally approved. The differences between the two programs lie chiefly in the coverage and in the source of revenue to finance the program.

The medical profession in this country has achieved a high technical and professional level and deserves every protection. Certainly doctors should be alert at all times to prevent any threat—not only any interference, but any serious threat to the practice of their profession. It has been argued that a national medical insurance program would control the way medicine is practiced by imposing standards on participating hospitals, would deny the patient free choice of hospital and doctor, and would intrude the government into the doctor-patient relationship. However, there is no good reason to believe that the practice of medicine would in any way be improperly controlled or influenced if this legislation were adopted.

The medical profession has had the strength to withstand a number of federal programs in the field of health and medicine—for example, the Veterans Hospital program, and the Hill-Burton Hospital construction program. It has withstood state medical aid programs, and group private efforts, such as the medical and hospital programs provided by large corporations and the Blue Cross insurance plans. All of these set up certain standards with regard to quality of treatment, facilities, hospital accreditation, and the like.

A final argument has arisen over how a program of hospital insurance should be financed if adopted, whether through a social security levy or by some other means.

The argument in favor of the social security approach as a means of financing the program is that medical aid lies in the general field of social insurance, and, in some respects, is similar to the Old Age and Survivors' Insurance program, commonly known as social security.

It is argued that the support of the medical program should not depend on the general revenues of the federal government. Senator Hartke, speaking on this question on August 20, 1960, said: "Frankly we feel the bill should be paid in the real American way, on an insurance basis by which individuals make contributions and later receive the benefits from their payments."

Walter Lippmann, in an article cited earlier in this chapter, stated the case somewhat more directly when he wrote: "There is nothing un-American in the principle that the imprudent shall be compelled to save so that they do not become a burden to their families and the local charities, so that they can meet the needs of their old age with the self-respect which comes with being entitled to the benefits because they have paid the cost out of their earnings."

Arguments against the social security approach are somewhat varied. Senator John Williams is representative of one group whose opposition is consistent with their general opposition to increased taxes. He has said that, "Surely we were not to witness the revival of the old New Deal philosophy of tax, spend, and elect. I am not unmindful of the fact that since we first put the federal income tax law into effect in 1913 there have been 15 tax increases and every one of these tax increases except two were enacted by the Democratic party. It is this free and easy tax and spending policy that distresses me. Some even argue that it does not make any difference how much we raise taxes just so long as we give something back to the people. If that is the program of this New Frontier coalition, I do not like it."

Other opponents of the social security approach argue that the costs should be met out of general revenue, which reflects the principle of the graduated income tax. This was the position of former Secretary of Health, Education, and Welfare, Mr. Flemming, when he appeared before the Finance Committee. This argument is something less than valid because a graduated scale would, in fact, be built into the method of paying for medical aid, even under the social security approach.

In the Old Age and Survivors' Insurance program, the benefits an individual receives are roughly related to the contribution which he makes and, of course, the amount of contribution is related to the income base upon which he pays, running from the first few hundred dollars subject to social security up to the current maximum of $4,800. The individual benefits vary accordingly, from a minimum of $40 a month up to $127.

The really important questions, then, are two: One, whether there is a need for such a program; and two, what is the best way of financing a program to meet this need. In passing judgment, one must weigh both the needs of the aged and the rights of the medical profession, and then proceed to the practical consideration of how the program should be financed.

If the social security concept is considered vital to the

program, then it should be tied in to social security. If it is accepted that this is a general need which should be met for the whole nation, then it could well be paid for out of general revenue in which the principle of payment on the basis of ability to pay would be reflected.

The only remaining practical question is whether or not the program should be extended to all persons or whether a means test should be included.

The medical aid bill for people over 65 should not be considered a relief bill, but rather a bill designed to strengthen the basic social structure of America. The people who would benefit are not social outcasts, not personal failures, but rather people who are the strength of America— its workers, its farmers, its small businessmen, its housewives. Born near the beginning of this century, most of them reached adulthood and were perhaps on the threshold of success when the depression of the Thirties struck.

These were persons who believed in the American dream— hard work in hope of success; who held that this was the land of opportunity. In the depression the small gains which many had made were destroyed and their hopes were disappointed. Then came recovery, but also World War II, and in many cases another interruption in their lives and in their efforts to achieve a measure of economic security.

At the same time, other significant changes had been taking place. One was the advance of medical science—the new drugs had extended the average life expectancy of our population from less than 50 years in 1900 to more than 70 today. In addition, changes in technology and the development of automation have served to displace workers earlier in life; have made it difficult within recent years for people over ages 45 or 50 to get employment, and consequently made it increasingly difficult for them to provide for their old age; and have made people over the age of 65 practically unemployable.

Along with these changes have been broad changes in the social structure of America as a result of which the old family and community units have been scattered, members of families—brothers and sisters—separated from one another and from their parents. The concentration of people in cities has made the aged person residing in the home nearly 100 percent dependent, a marked change from the days when older people living in rural communities and on the farm could perform useful services for the family. All of these changes and developments must be taken into account in the consideration of the need for legislation.

The great majority—up to 80 or 90 percent—of those

70

over 65 have special problems in meeting their medical expenses. These people have made a contribution to the building of America, and they are deserving of our consideration and our help. The case has been very well put by Senator Humphrey, who has said, "We must protect our aged and elderly citizens against the crushing catastrophic financial burden of serious illness and health care, and free them from nagging anxiety, from demoralizing fear that even brief illness may wipe out the savings of a lifetime overnight, leaving behind poverty and destitution and helpless dependence on public relief after the illness is past.

"Health benefits," he continued, "can and should be included with social security benefits. Not as an act of charity, but as an earned right just as social security pensions are an earned right, earned by a lifetime of contributions during the working year. Who will deny that unmet health needs exist among our senior citizens?" (August 22, 1960, *Congressional Record*)

☆☆☆ *Chapter 3*
THE KEYSTONE IN FREEDOM'S ARCH

The last four Presidents—Truman, Eisenhower, Kennedy and Johnson—have asked for greater federal participation in financing education in the United States.

In his message on education of January 29, 1963, President Kennedy said that, "At the turn of the century, only 10 percent of our adults had a high school or college education. Today such an education has become a requirement for an increasing number of jobs. . . . Our education system faces a major problem of quantity—of coping with the needs of our expanding population and of the rising educational expectations for our children which all of us share as parents. Nearly 50 million people were enrolled in our schools and colleges in 1962—an increase of more than 50 percent since 1950. By 1970, college enrollment will nearly double, and secondary schools will increase enrollment by 50 percent. . . . Now a veritable tidal wave of students is advancing inexorably on our institutions of higher education, where the annual costs per student are several times as high as the cost of a high school education, and where these costs must be borne in large part by the student or his parents. Five years ago the graduating class of the secondary schools was 1.5 million; five years from now it will be 2.5 million." Many students from families with low incomes cannot manage to meet these high costs.

The President further declared that, "Total national outlays for education nearly trebled during the 1940's and more than doubled during the 1950's, reaching a level of nearly $25 billion in 1960. As a proportion of national income, this represented a rise from little more than 4 percent in 1940 to nearly 6 percent in 1960, an increase of over 40 percent in total effort."

Changes and trends such as these moved the late Senator Robert Taft to change his position from one of opposition to federal aid to one of support. In 1939 he said, "If there is any activity in which the people are able to stand on their own feet without being nursed from Washington, education is that activity. . . ." But in 1948 he said, "Four years ago, I opposed the then pending bill on this subject, but in the course of that debate it became so apparent that many children in the United States were left without education. . . . I feel strongly that in the fields of education, health, housing and relief, the federal government has a secondary obligation. . . . In my judgment the important thing is to avoid direct federal action. . . . If we can work out an effective state aid system which will leave the administration in the states I believe we can escape the danger of concentration and can remain merely an auxiliary assisting power rather than an actual operating power."

It is estimated that the costs of elementary and secondary education alone will be approximately $31 to $32 billion by 1970. States and local communities are finding it more and more difficult to bear the costs of education. According to the Rockefeller Report, the percentage of school support coming from state governments increased from about 17 percent in 1930 to over 37 percent in 1954. The costs of education must be met from some source: parents, nongovernmental group efforts, local or state government, the federal government, or by combinations of some or all of these.

In theory, responsibility for the basic education of children rests in the family. Parents have an obligation to educate their children either by their own effort or through tutors or schools, if these are available or can be made available. Every developing society is quick to manifest community responsibility for the education of the young. So in the United States, in the colonial settlements and in pioneer communities, one of the first common efforts was

72

to establish common schools. In new suburbs today, one of the first common concerns is for education. Local and parental responsibility has continued, but burdens have been shifted or extended to include states and, in some fields of education, the federal government, or, more properly, the total national community.

Although there are a few in the extremist groups in the United States who argue against any community support of education, criticism and opposition are most commonly directed against what is called "federal aid to education." Senator Goldwater declares quite flatly that federal aid is unconstitutional. In the *Saturday Review*, March 18, 1961, he wrote: "There can be no question but that federal intervention in our educational system through aid programs is unconstitutional. . . . Education is one of the powers reserved to the states by the 10th Amendment to the Constitution."

Few constitutional authorities support this opinion, nor do many of those who endorse it extend it far beyond elementary and secondary levels.

Federal participation in support of education in the United States is not new or revolutionary. The federal government has been involved in the support of education for 175 years. Four years before the adoption of the Constitution, in the Survey Ordinance of 1785, the national government provided that "there shall be reserved the lot #16 of every township for the maintenance of public schools in each township." The Northwest Ordinance of 1787 contained a similar provision.

The Morrill Acts of 1862 and 1890 created a system of land grant colleges. And direct federal aid to vocational education was provided in the Smith-Hughes Act of 1917. More than 3 million World War II and Korean conflict veterans have received $6 billion in federal funds since 1944 to assist them to attend college. The National Defense Education Act's college student loan program has aided more than 300,000 students in more than 1,500 institutions, who have borrowed nearly $220 million. Fifteen hundred fellowships are authorized annually under the National Defense Education Act. The needs today are unusual in that there are both quantitative and qualitative pressures for improved and expanded educational effort.

It is clear that the community, acting through governmental agencies, has a responsibility in the field of education. The state as an institution concerned primarily with the temporal good of man has a right and an obligation to set up standards for education, and the right to require its

73

citizens to meet these standards insofar as it is possible for them to do so. The standards must, of course, be reasonable and must leave open great areas of freedom for the pursuit of truth and individual fulfillment.

If individuals alone, or children with the aid of their parents, are not able to achieve these minimum standards, the state has a responsibility to assist, if it can, in the effort to develop the full potential of each member of society. This does not imply the acceptance of an egalitarian philosophy, for the objective is egalitarian only in the sense that it seeks to give each person an equal chance, not to be like everyone else, but to become fully himself.

There can be no serious distinction on a theoretical basis between aid to education by local or state governmental units and aid by the federal government. The question of whether federal aid should be provided or not is a practical one.

In 1958 the Rockefeller Report pointed out that state and local tax revenues were no longer adequate. "In the past," the report stated, "Americans have preferred to accomplish the financing of public education . . . at the state and local level. But state and local tax systems are in some respects archaic and it is very difficult to keep the revenue from these sources growing in step with the economy or with the growing demand for governmental services which an expanding economy creates. This is due partly to the excessive dependence . . . upon the real property tax, which is notably laggard in its response to rising income, and it is due partly to the fact that state and local governments are reluctant to extend or expand these taxing systems for fear of placing the communities or states at a competitive disadvantage." Add to this the fact that the wide variation in personal income among the states is generally reflected in poorer educational facilities in low-income states.

A popular argument against federal participation is that it would be accompanied by unwarranted and dangerous federal intervention in the educational system. Russell Kirk, one spokesman for conservatives, stated this position in the *National Review*, February 25, 1961: "What the zealots for federal aid really desire is not simply more money but more power. The present pretexts of school construction and bonuses to teachers' salaries are intended merely as entering wedges: the first steps toward establishing a wholly centralized system of public instruction, directed by an important Washington bureaucracy. And that bureaucracy would be formed of ideologues whose god is John Dewey, intent on smashing traditional education and substituting

74

'progressive,' 'permissive' life adjustment collectivistic educational dogmas."

It is, of course, impossible to read the minds and determine the real intent of all those who advocate federal aid to education. Some may have in mind what Kirk suspects. The safer and fairer judgment, however, is that most of the advocates of aid are seeking a practical means of meeting what they believe to be a pressing problem.

Dr. Sterling McMurrin, Commissioner of Education for the United States until his resignation in 1962, disagrees with Mr. Kirk. "I do not believe," he wrote in *The Saturday Evening Post*, March 23, 1963, "giving more federal funds to public schools will lead to federal control of public education, for the simple reason that no one wants it. The educators don't want it, the taxpayers don't want it, and quite certainly the people in government don't want it."

Federal aid would, of course, involve application of some minimum standards; certainly the federal aid would have to be used for education. The National Defense Education Act, for example, requires that colleges contribute one dollar to student loan funds for every nine dollars contributed by the federal government. It provides for preference in granting loans to students "with a superior capacity or preparation in science, mathematics, engineering or modern foreign language," and also provides for loan forgiveness of up to 50 percent for teaching in a public elementary or secondary school.

It requires that states match federal funds for the purchase of teaching aids and laboratory equipment on a dollar for dollar basis. It authorizes federal aid to state educational agencies to improve supervision of teaching, but only in the science, mathematics, and modern foreign language fields. It provides for a program of graduate fellowships, but only to colleges which start new graduate programs or expand existing ones which "substantially further the objective of increasing the facilities available in the nation for the graduate training of college or university level teachers and of promoting a wider geographical distribution of such facilities."

In this case and on the general record, federal participation has not resulted in undue interference or domination of state or local education or of private education.

While it is correct to say in the abstract that government should do for its citizens only what they cannot do for themselves, or do as well, in the practical situation it may sometimes be necessary for government to do things because persons or subsidiary groups cannot do things as effectively or as quickly as they need to be done, or because persons and other groups do not do the things and either cannot or should not be required to do so.

In his book *What I Think,* Adlai Stevenson remarks that, "In a real sense the central issue of education is . . . how a civilization which has reached, at least in America, unprecedented heights of material well-being and unlocked awesome secrets of the physical world is also to master the ways for preserving its spiritual and moral and intellectual values." He goes on to say that, "In a narrower, more political sense the issue of education is how democracy can be made an instrument by which people work together to mobilize the strength of the community to fight ignorance as effectively as we have fought every other enemy which has threatened us."

President Kennedy stressed the importance of education to the nation in his 1963 message on education when he said: "For the individual, the doors to the schoolhouse, to the library and to the college lead to the richest treasures of our open society: to the power of knowledge—to the training and skills necessary for productive employment—to the wisdom, the ideals, and the culture which enrich life—and to the creative, self-disciplined understanding of society needed for good citizenship in today's changing and challenging world. Education is the keystone in the arch of freedom and progress. Nothing has contributed more to the enlargement of this nation's strength and opportunities than our traditional system of free, universal elementary and secondary education, coupled with widespread availability of college education. For the nation, increasing the quality and availability of education is vital to both our national security and our domestic well-being."

These are compelling arguments for better education and certainly indicate a need for federal participation. We cannot afford an inadequate educational system; nor should we be kept from providing one by unsound arguments—theoretical or historical.

☆☆☆ Chapter 4
FREEDOM TO BE EQUAL

The search for freedom and for a world in which freedom might be enjoyed has been the preoccupation of civilized people throughout the history of the world. This seeking for freedom has characterized every culture from the most primitive to the most civilized and has been manifested many times by those who have shown heroic willingness to settle in most hostile environments—jungles, mountains, deserts—in order to preserve their identity as a people and to be free from those restraints which they considered to be obstacles to their freedom and happiness.

In the famous Four Freedoms address of January 6, 1941, Franklin Roosevelt gave the world a triumphant list of freedoms to be held to in the face of the totalitarian threat.

"We look forward," he said, "to a world founded upon four essential human freedoms. The first is freedom of speech and expression—everywhere in the world. The second is freedom of every person to worship God in his own way—everywhere in the world. The third is freedom from want, which translated into world terms means economic understandings which will secure to every nation a healthy, peaceful life for its inhabitants—everywhere in the world. The fourth is freedom from fear—anywhere in the world."

Whereas the particular danger to these freedoms is different today from what it was in 1941, and different in the United States from what it is in other parts of the world, the challenge is the same, and these freedoms still stand as the first line of objectives which good men seek throughout the world. Our continuing problem is to undertake to establish basic conditions of certainty and stability and that limited measure of security which is necessary for the growth and flowering of freedom, and to eliminate, insofar as we can, all those things which push man toward evil and inhumanity.

The Constitution of the United States attempted to define the measure of governmental responsibility and at the same time to define certain areas of civil liberties: individual freedom and freedom of institutions within society. This is the concept of limited government, quite different from Plato's idea that the role of government is not only to secure

77

justice and order but to instill all virtues—intellectual, moral, and physical—and to restrain all vices.

The First Amendment to the Constitution is an affirmation of civil liberties and also of personal liberties. It describes and defines certain areas in which no restrictive laws are to intrude. The development of constitutional law in our courts has shown a continuing concern to protect these basic liberties. At the same time there has been manifest a recognition of the responsibility of government to help to establish conditions and means which enable citizens to enjoy these liberties in greater measure.

The regard for civil liberties and the defense of these liberties is not the work of government alone. It is a work in which every citizen and every civic, religious, and educational organization has responsibilities. The danger of subordination of individuals or minorities to the will of the majority has been offset principally by our emphasis on individual rights, our insistence on tolerance of nonconformity, and the support and freedom and measure of authority we give to nongovernment agencies.

There is, of course, an extensive, unmarked area within which functions which are properly the duty of government and those from which government should be excluded cannot always be clearly separated. There is a broad range calling for prudential determination, in which action may be justified temporarily or contingently, as in Justice Holmes's ruling regarding restriction of freedom of speech on the basis of "clear and present danger" to the public safety.

The need for government action is of two kinds: positive or negative, supporting or protective.

Senator Goldwater has said that, "The only civil right that is mentioned in the Constitution is the right to vote . . . as of now, we have one civil right and we have taken care of it. That is the right to vote."

The basic civil liberties guaranteed by the Constitution and emphasized in it are many: freedom of speech, freedom of religion, freedom of assembly, the right to privacy, prohibition against quartering of troops and search without warrant, the right to vote, trial by jury, and equality before the laws.

Civil rights are not the same as human rights. Human rights do not arise from law; rather, they arise from the nature of man, or rest in that nature. The determination and definition of human rights is a problem of philosophy. There is a need to determine which rights are properly subject to civil control, both positive and negative, and to determine also how these rights can be secured and exercised.

In the United States many fundamental human rights are also civil rights, since they are guaranteed and protected by the Constitution and by law. These are the rights expressly or implicitly protected by the Constitution of the United States, extended and clarified by court decisions, by tradition, and by statute. Every citizen is included except those who have forfeited citizenship temporarily, as in the case of criminals, or permanently, as in the case of expatriates, or those from whom, for some reason, citizenship has been withdrawn.

Freedom of speech, so essential to democracy, is based not so much upon the right of every person to speak or to print as it is upon the need and the right of every person to seek and to apprehend the truth. A practical guarantee to insure this is to allow those who believe that they possess the truth to speak out.

We do not recognize in this country the right of anyone to say anything he wishes. A standard example is the denial of the right of a man to shout "fire" in a crowded theater. Nonetheless, as we move from such obvious things as the interpretation of history to questions of philosophy and theological beliefs, and even to some areas of morality, the disposition of the government to intrude, to interfere, and to control should be most carefully guarded against. And not only the disposition of government, but that of other centers which have power to control thought: educational institutions, newspapers, magazines, libraries, radio and television.

Religious liberty, too, is realized, although in this area also there has been restrictive action, principally in the limitations set upon the Mormon Church in its practice of polygamy, which was forbidden as a matter of public policy, and occasional action against extremist religious groups who practice physical violence upon their members. A more serious problem in the United States is to prevent a kind of closing in upon religious groups in the name of religious liberty.

Freedom of assembly is generally recognized in principle, but when practiced in such actions as picketing or mass demonstrations is subject to some restraint in fact and to demands for greater restraint.

The right to trial by jury, of course, is acknowledged. Arguments arise, however, with reference to such things as providing counsel, financial support of trials, police methods, undue detention, and the like.

Such obvious things as the forbidding of quartering of troops and the right to privacy are recognized. A somewhat less careful line is drawn in various proposals for search without warrant and for wiretapping.

Rights are not realized in a vacuum. This is not a society of free or perfect men. In some cases, substantive rights are practically meaningless without procedural protection, methods of appeal, and methods of seeking redress.

The conservative position on civil rights is one of many contradictions. Usually the conservatives are outspoken and quick to act when questions of property rights are involved. On questions of freedom of speech, of religion, of assembly, and of the right to privacy, they are commonly on the side of those who advocate more governmental intervention and restraint. Part of their difficulty is ideological.

Russell Kirk, in a book entitled *The Intelligent Woman's Guide to Conservatism,* states that "The wise government, in the conservative's view, tries to ensure two great principles relative to human personality. The first of these principles is that the men and women of remarkable minds and abilities ought to be protected in their right to develop and unfold their unusual personalities. The second of these principles is that the men and women in the ordinary walks of life, who do not have the ability or the wish to accomplish remarkable things, ought to be protected in their right to proceed in the placid round of their duties and enjoyments. . . ."

One group, it seems, is to be set free; the other, to be protected.

Peter Viereck, in his book *Conservatism Revisited,* presents the same case in somewhat more theoretical terms. "In one sense," he says, "the concept of civil liberties is aristocratic and against democratic rule. . . . Guarding the Bill of Rights even against majorities and even against the peoples' will, the American Constitution performs an aristocratic and conservative function."

Certainly the Bill of Rights seeks to preserve basic civil liberties, and in so doing fulfills a conservative function. The threat may not be the peoples' will, the will of the ordinary people described by Russell Kirk, but may be the will of those making up Viereck's aristocracy—a potential majority.

A working concept of civil rights cannot include arbitrary class or group distinctions. Of course, the Constitution of the United States, when first adopted, did not fully reflect the promise of equality affirmed to be self-evident in the Declaration of Independence. It had to be amended and clarified by court decisions. In some respects it remains imperfect today.

The adoption of the Constitution hinged on compromises. Slavery was recognized, and slaves were excluded from citizenship. Under the terms of the three-fifths compromise, the humanity of slaves was recognized to a degree, since they were counted in part to determine the number of representatives to be given to each state in the House of Representatives. Slavery was not abolished, but it was agreed that the slave trade would be abolished after 1808.

The fact is that this issue could not be settled by legislation or by other governmental action within the framework of law one hundred years ago, but became the breaking point in the Civil War and remains the breaking point today. The proposition of equality is not debatable. Those who oppose equality in practice must, and in too many cases are prepared to, do so by violence—physical in some cases, in other cases by nonphysical opposition—in their manifest willingness to frustrate and obstruct the workings of law and justice.

The reversal—or, better, the correction—by the Supreme Court of the "separate but equal" rule established by the *Plessy v. Ferguson* decision in 1896 requires full application of the 14th Amendment, which forbids any state from making or enforcing any law which shall abridge the privileges or immunities of citizens of the United States, or shall deprive any person of life, liberty or property without due process of law, or deny to any person within the state's jurisdiction the equal protection of the law.

The Court has acknowledged that discrimination is more fundamental than differences in quality of transportation or of educational facilities, or other differences in services or in equipment which people may use. Segregation on purely physical or racial standards is, in itself, the basic act of discrimination.

The consequences of discrimination are everywhere evident, but most clearly in the case of Negroes. The median income of Negro families is about 50 percent that of white families. In 1961 Negroes made up 21 percent of the unemployed, although they made up only 11 percent of the working force. Automation and advances in technology hit Negroes particularly hard because the majority of them are unskilled. Less than one percent of the apprentices in the construction trades are Negroes.

Negroes experience greater difficulty in obtaining financing for the purchase of homes than do whites, especially if they wish to buy in a better area. In general their housing is substandard and overcrowded. In part this reflects economic status. It also reflects the suburban pressure against sales to Negroes and the pressure resulting from the decay of urban centers and subsequent urban renewal, which forces Negroes in many cities into a compressed area or belt.

A 1961 report of the Civil Rights Commission stated that

Negroes were being prevented from voting in 100 counties in the southern states.

Negroes have been excluded from the best universities and colleges in the South. Their elementary schools and secondary schools have generally been below prevailing standards of the communities and states.

In the face of these facts, governmental action has been called for and is being called for today by liberals. Conservatives generally have opposed such action or have been indifferent to it.

Twelve Republican Presidents have served in office during the past 100 years without initiating one single major piece of civil rights legislation; nor has a Republican President been responsible for a single new administrative regulation which sought to secure equal opportunities for every United States citizen. There have been two Congresses in the last thirty years which were controlled in both the House and the Senate by Republican majorities: the 80th Congress in 1947-48 and the 83rd in 1953-54, during President Eisenhower's Administration. Neither of these Congresses passed any civil rights legislation.

This lack of action is not accidental; it is the expression of conservative opinion. Thus William Buckley, writing in the *Saturday Review* in November 11, 1961, declared: "What, I am asked, is the conservative's solution to the race problem in the South. I answer: there is no present solution to it. . . . A conservative," he states in the same article, "is seldom disposed to use the federal government as a sword of social justice, for the sword is generally two-edged. It is doubtful just what enduring benefits the Southern Negro would receive from the intervention of government . . . it is less doubtful what the consequences of integration would be to the ideal of local government and the sense of community ideals which I am not ready to abandon, not even to kill Jim Crow."

Senator Goldwater, in his book *The Conscience of a Conservative,* writes: "The federal Constitution does *not* require the States to maintain racially mixed schools. . . . It may be just or wise or expedient for Negro children to attend the same schools as white children, but they do not have a civil right to do so which is protected by the federal Constitution, or which is enforceable by the federal government. . . . Under the 10th Amendment, jurisdiction [over education] was reserved to the States. . . . The [14th] amendment was not intended to and therefore it did not outlaw racially separate schools. It was not intended to, and therefore it did not, authorize *any* federal intervention in the field of education."

Contrast with these views and record of inaction, liberal

views and the positive action of administrations called liberal, and note the results.

Franklin Roosevelt established a civil rights section in the Department of Justice in 1939 and a Committee on Fair Employment Practices in 1941. Executive orders were issued in 1941 and 1943, prohibiting discrimination by any company holding defense contracts.

In July 1948 President Truman set up a Fair Employment Practices Board in the Civil Service Commission to review complaints of discrimination. The Truman Administration was the first to seek full federal entry into the civil rights field, with a comprehensive legislative program including anti-lynch, anti-poll tax, and anti-segregation laws and the establishment of a Fair Employment Practices Commission. An executive order of President Truman in 1948 established a policy of "equality of treatment and opportunity for all persons in the armed services without regard to race, color, religion or national origin."

Until the summer of 1963 the Kennedy Administration did not exert any strong pressure for civil rights legislation, but had stressed executive action to accomplish the same objectives. An executive order of March 6, 1961 created the President's Committee on Equal Employment Opportunity, which initiated a vigorous program intended to eliminate discrimination in employment in government agencies and by contractors and sub-contractors doing business with the government or any of its departments or agencies.

On May 31, 1961, the Secretary of the Interior issued an anti-discrimination regulation covering national park facilities. On April 13, 1961, the Postmaster General announced that all advertisements for bids to build postal facilities and all leases negotiated by postal authorities must contain non-discrimination clauses.

From January 1, 1961 to 1963, the Department of Justice filed 23 suits to assert and defend voting rights under the civil rights acts of 1957 and 1960. In 1960-61 the Department of Justice intervened as *amicus curiae* in four suits to protect the processes and orders of the federal district court which had directed desegregation of New Orleans public schools. The department also intervened in the Tuskegee gerrymandering case and in the New Rochelle school case. An executive order on Equal Opportunity in Housing was issued on November 20, 1962.

Court rulings have also contributed significantly to the clarification of the constitutional rights of all persons in the United States.

The *Plessy v. Ferguson* case of 1896, although concerned with intrastate railroad transportation, established the general "separate but equal" principle which came to be applied to education.

Following *Plessy v. Ferguson,* there were six cases involving the "separate but equal" doctrine as applied to public education. In two cases the validity of the doctrine was not challenged; in the ensuing four, all in the realm of higher education, facilities were found to be, in fact, unequal.

As a result of these later decisions by the Supreme Court, and other decisions in lower courts, the barriers began to crumble in the field of higher education in the 1930's and the 1940's. Between 1935 and 1959, 124 of 195 formerly all-white tax-supported colleges in the southern and border states and the District of Columbia abandoned segregation. Nearly 100 of this number took such action after the 1954 Court decision. By 1954, state universities had opened their doors to Negroes everywhere but in Mississippi, Alabama, Georgia, Florida, and South Carolina.

The Supreme Court decision of 1954 (*Brown v. Topeka Board of Education*) stated that "to separate children from others of similar age and qualifications solely because of their race generates a feeling of inferiority as to their status in the community that may affect their hearts and minds in a way unlikely to be undone." Thus the 1954 decision established the principle that segregated schools are inherently unequal and therefore a violation of the equal protection clause of the 14th Amendment.

The way had been prepared for this broad decision by earlier higher education cases and by a series of decisions from the time of World War I in which the Court struck down state and local laws which discriminated against Negroes in such fields as voting, housing, and transportation.

There was no significant legislative action in the field of civil rights in over 80 years until the passage of the Civil Rights Act of 1957. The Senate made two major amendments to this bill as it passed the House: It eliminated the section which would have permitted the Attorney General to institute civil action for preventive relief in civil rights cases and, in effect, limited the bill to the enforcement of voting rights only; and it added the jury trial amendment, which guaranteed jury trials in all criminal contempt cases —not only those arising out of this bill—with the judge retaining the right to rule without a jury in cases of civil contempt.

The House and Senate ultimately agreed on a compromise version of the jury trial amendment. The compromise, which applied only to voting rights cases, permitted judges to try minor criminal contempt cases without a jury, but assured a defendant a new trial by jury when the penalty imposed by the judge was more than $300 or 45 days in jail.

When the 86th Congress convened in January 1959, the question of new civil rights legislation loomed large. The Commission on Civil Rights had gotten off to a slow start and had run into a number of legal challenges in its efforts to investigate denial of voting rights, and, therefore, the need was felt to extend its life beyond the deadline of September 9, 1959.

In addition, the Civil Rights Division of the Department of Justice had been encountering difficulties in its efforts to enforce voting rights. Only one suit had been brought by the time the 86th Congress convened, and that suit was dismissed by the District Court on the grounds that the 1957 Act was unconstitutional. This action was later reversed by the Supreme Court in 1960, but the need for further legislation had been demonstrated.

Moreover, the controversy over school desegregation had not abated, and there was a need for some sort of congressional affirmation of support for the Court decision and also for action to restrain mob violence and bombings of schools, churches, and homes.

The Civil Rights Act of 1960 provided that persons who obstructed or interfered with any order of a federal court by threats or force could be punished by a fine of up to $1,000 or imprisonment up to one year or both, and provided for private suits to seek court injunctions against such action. The Act made it a federal crime to transport or possess explosives with knowledge or intent that they would be used for bombings. It required the preservation of voting records and registration papers for all federal elections for 22 months and directed that the records be turned over to the Attorney General upon his written application.

It also permitted the Attorney General to ask the court to make a finding that there was a "pattern or practice" of depriving Negroes of the right to vote in a given area after he had won a suit regarding voting rights brought under the 1957 Act. Given this finding, any Negro in the area who had been refused registration could apply to the court to issue an order declaring him qualified to vote. The courts were also empowered to appoint voting referees to receive applications, take evidence, and report findings to the court, and state officials were subject to contempt of court for disobeying an order to permit voting.

The 87th Congress extended and strengthened the Civil

Rights Commission and approved a constitutional amendment to outlaw poll taxes in federal elections, the amendment to take effect when ratified by 38 states.

Court decisions, executive orders, and legislation approved by the Congress have not eliminated all discrimination. A government cannot run far ahead of general prejudices and habits if its orders or laws are to be fully effective. We cannot repeal prejudice by law, yet law is more than educational, and it should run ahead of prejudice.

The injustice of segregation is so great and so clear, and the reduction and elimination of discrimination so vital to democracy, that recourse to law, to the courts and to public action, is necessary.

☆☆☆ *Chapter 5*

THE POLITICS OF PROCEDURE

There is in the United States a growing concern over the operation of government. Some observers fear that the balance of power between the executive branch of government and the legislative branch has been upset; others charge that the judicial branch has usurped the powers of the legislative branch; still others contend that the federal government is encroaching on areas which should be reserved to state and local governments. There is a widespread and growing demand for reform of the rules and procedures of the Congress of the United States.

Of course, one must be concerned about the effectiveness of the methods and procedures in democratic government, for democracy is never self-operating. On the other hand, the best rules and procedures cannot of themselves make democracy vital and effective.

The men who drafted the Constitution did not anticipate a complete separation in which the Congress would be the policy-making body and the President's function would be limited to the execution of laws. The President was given the right to recommend such measures as he judged necessary and expedient, and he was also given the veto power.

The problem of maintaining a proper balance and control reflects historical changes. The executive branch has been given the authority to spend over $90 billion a year. It has been necessary for the Congress to delegate to the executive the power to make administrative rules which come to have the effect of law. The departments of the executive branch have immense discretionary power in administering the laws. The Congress takes the responsibility for making laws, but once a law is passed or funds appropriated, the Congress has little control except through an occasional investigating committee.

My concern is not with the letter of the Constitution so much as with the question of representative government: with the intention which, I think, is clear on the part of the men who drafted the Constitution, that the representatives of the people should share in major policy-making. Procedures for involving the Congress in decision-making through the device of the joint committee or other innovations are, I believe, vital to the future.

The need, in very general terms, runs in two directions: One, in the direction of giving either more authority or more discretion in the use of authority to the President in such fields as public finance, expenditures, taxation, foreign trade and other questions of foreign policy; the other in the direction of involving the Congress more directly and more intimately in foreign policy decisions in such areas of foreign affairs as intelligence activities, space exploration, and decisions relating to the domestic economy.

In recent years most discussion has related to two major changes in procedures of Congress: one, to change the Rules Committee of the House of Representatives; and two, to limit debate in the Senate.

For the most part liberals—both Democrats and Republicans, in and outside of the Congress—are asking for these and other changes, whereas conservatives are generally opposed to changes in the rules.

The conservative position on the filibuster rule, known as Rule XXII of the Senate, is essentially that stated by Senator Russell in a speech which was recorded in the *Congressional Record* of January 14, 1963, and also by Senator Thurmond, speaking for the *Record* of February 4, 1963. In the debate on the Senate rules change, Senator Russell said:

> "Those of us who oppose the proposed changes in the rules are not looking only to civil rights legislation. We are looking also to the protection of the proud position of the Senate, and its unique role in our scheme of government.
> "We are undertaking to defend the individual rights and prerogatives of Members of this body. We cannot liquidate the power of the Senate with-

out liquidating the power of every individual Senator. We cannot water down the power of the Senate without weakening the power and prestige of every individual Senator.

"The Senate is the last place of refuge of small States and minorities. The small States of the Nation have no other place in our political or government life where they can make their presence felt. . . .

"Mr. President, there is no question that the rules of the Senate can be changed by the Senate in the manner prescribed by the rules. I am insisting on orderly procedure, in order that the Senate may maintain its proud position, rather than begin to take shortcuts to avoid or evade the rules. If my friends were to succeed in avoiding or evading the rules, they would soon see rushed through the Senate all kinds of legislation that would not have anything to do with civil rights, unless it would be to impinge upon the right of private property; or they would see rushed through the Senate legislation that would not even be called civil rights legislation. No doubt that would include legislation to change the economy of the country without giving Senators an opportunity to stand on their feet and inveigh against it.

"If the rules of the Senate were to be changed in so extraordinary a fashion, the Senate itself would be threatened; and the Senate is the most powerful single instrumentality of Government which exists. Emasculate the powers of the Senate and the whole fabric of our Government would soon be torn and destroyed."

Senator Thurmond stated his position later in the same debate:

"Mr. President, this attack upon the rules of the U.S. Senate should be viewed as what it really is— a frontal assault upon tradition and orderly procedure and a real and present danger to the Senate of the United States. This fact is largely forgotten or intentionally overlooked due to the propaganda barrage leveled against the present rule XXII by the liberal press as merely a device for defeating civil rights legislation. Nothing could be further from the truth.

88

"Tradition, in and of itself, is not sacred and cannot provide the complete answer to every problem. Nevertheless, long-standing traditions are seldom maintained without sufficient reason. Almost invariably, traditions serve as a warning beacon of oft forgotten and sometimes obscure, but always sound and logical purposes.

"A beacon of more than 170 years' unbroken tradition stands as a warning of the seriousness of the proposal before this body. Should the motion to proceed to a consideration of the rules be favorably considered by this body, this 170-year tradition will be destroyed, and regardless of a subsequent return to the same method of procedure by this body after sober reflection, the tradition will be broken, and the beacon extinguished forever.

"Even more vital, however, are the logical purposes which prompted the unshattered existence of this tradition. Foremost among these purposes is that of insuring an orderly procedure, so vital in such an authoritative body."

The argument of conservatives is essentially an argument against majority rule. The men who drafted the Constitution were, of course, concerned with the arbitrary rule of the majority and did attempt to set up some defenses for the minority. The ultimate defense was that provided for in the Constitution itself, primarily in the Bill of Rights—with the minority, and ultimately every individual person, having the right to the protection of the courts. Small states are protected by the provision that each state, no matter what its population, shall have the same number of senators. Action in international relations conducted through treaties was to be approved by at least a two-thirds vote of the Senate.

Basic to the operation of the legislative branch of the government is, however, rule by majority vote. Frustrating the majority by prolonged debate was in no way sustained or supported at the Constitutional Convention. Yet the fact is that the technique of prolonged debate, or filibuster, has been effective in frustrating the majority of the Congress of the United States. Since 1917, when the Senate authorized the limitation of debate by two-thirds of those present and voting, cloture has been moved 27 times and has failed 22 times. It has failed every time when it was invoked with reference to civil rights—some 11 times.

The liberal argument against the filibuster is the simple one that after adequate debate on a matter which is properly a legislative one, which is subject to all the protection of the veto and appeal to the Supreme Court, and which has been considered in an orderly way, the intention and decision of the majority should be determined. The rights of the minority are fully recognized when they have been heard and have had their point of view presented and expressed in debate and through a vote.

Alexander Hamilton, writing in *The Federalist*, No. 22, strongly emphasized this point as follows: "To give a minority a negative upon a majority (which is always the case where more than a majority is requisite to a decision), is, in its tendency, to subject the sense of the greater number to that of the lesser. . . . If a pertinacious minority can control the opinion of a majority, respecting the best mode of conducting it, the majority, in order that something may be done, must conform to the views of the minority; and thus the sense of the smaller number will overrule that of the greater, and give a tone to the national proceedings."

This mood was reflected in the Constitution, which prescribed majority rule as the rule of Congressional action with five exceptions, two of which have been referred to above. These five are in connection with the power of the Congress to override the veto, senatorial ratification of treaties, initiation in the Congress of proposals to amend the Constitution, the impeachment power, and the expulsion of members of Congress. Majority rule is the constitutional measure for legislative action.

In the House of Representatives the procedural fight has centered around the Rules Committee, which has the responsibility for determining the time and the conditions under which legislative matters shall be submitted for debate and action on the floor of the House. The dispute usually concerns the question whether or not the membership of that committee should be increased to a point where the majority position of the majority party of the Congress is clearly represented on the committee.

The case against such change was made by Republican conservative leaders rather clearly in the 1961 debate recorded for the *Congressional Record* of January 31. Congressman Clarence Brown of Ohio, ranking Republican Rules Committee member, had this to say:

"If the Rules Committee is packed it will be possible for those in control to withhold from or send to the floor for action any and all legislation. More sinister and dangerous is the fact it will be possible for the committee to report any closed or gag rule desired, so as to prevent members from offering amendments to a bill, or otherwise work their will thereon. Rules could also be reported to waive points of order, so any given bill could carry provisions otherwise contrary to House rules, and even to statutory law. If the Rules Committee can be packed to obtain political decisions, other committees of the House can likewise be packed. . . . There is no reason to believe that the Rules Committee, as now constituted, will or can prevent any important legislation from receiving consideration by the House, for the House of Representatives can always work its will on legislative matters. . . . The majority leadership already have the means and the powers to bring any legislation before the House for consideration. Such have long been exercised."

Congressman Charles Halleck, Minority Leader, supported this position:

"I know because I have worked there that the Committee on Rules performs a most constructive service for the Members of this body and for the people of this country. I am submitting that the Committee on Rules time and again has responded by granting rules that individual members of the committee did not want; and I know by experience, I have observed, that a determined majority leadership can get action in the Committee on Rules and can get measures to the floor if it wants to. Certainly the Committee on Rules is not obligated to report to this floor every bill that comes before it; and as I look around I see members who I am quite sure are thankful for that. At the same time, it is not the province of the Committee on Rules to roadblock legislation that ought to be seriously considered. The safeguards against such indiscriminate action are well known."

The question was not whether to abolish the Rules Committee, which performs a useful function in granting rules and establishing conditions under which debate shall be carried on, but rather whether or not the Rules Committee should be an effective instrument of the majority party or, at least, of the majority of the majority party. Certainly it seems little to ask in a Congressional system such as ours

91

that the majority party, or those who are the majority in that party, should at least be strengthened to the point of being able to present their program to the House of Representatives under reasonably favorable conditions. All of the basic rules of debate in the House and the determination by majority vote, of course, would apply to any legislation which was considered, since the Rules Committee could do no more than determine limited conditions under which programs, resolutions, and bills would be presented for discussion and for action.

The case for making the Rules Committee an instrument for the majority was made effectively by those who spoke for a change. These included Speaker Sam Rayburn, Congressman Paul Kilday of Texas, Majority Leader John McCormack, Congressman Sidney Yates of Illinois, and Congressman John Blatnik of Minnesota.

Speaker Rayburn said: "I think this House should be allowed on great measures to work its will, and it cannot work its will if the Committee on Rules is so constituted as not to allow the House to pass on those things."

Congressman Kilday pointed out that: "The Committee on Rules is an arm of the leadership of the majority party. The majority party has the responsibility of the legislative program of the House. The majority party has the right to bring to the floor of the House the legislative proposals of the Committees. Once a proposal is on the floor, each member is a free agent to consider, to decide, and to vote as he sees fit. Because of this traditional organization one who assumes membership on the Committee on Rules must be prepared to exercise a function of leadership. His personal objection to the proposal is not always sufficient reason for him to vote to deny the membership of the whole House the opportunity to express its approval, or, equally important, the opportunity to express its disapproval."

Majority Leader John McCormack of Massachusetts contended that the change was "entirely a procedural matter."

Congressman Yates said that, "Over the years, this committee has frustrated the will of the majority by refusing to grant rules on major legislation or by insisting that bills pending before it be amended in substantial respects as conditions to the granting of a rule. These are privileges which were never given nor intended to be given to the committee, for the Committee on Rules is supposed to be a traffic artery, not a dead end street. Passage of this resolution will not destroy the function of the Rules Committee. Rather, it will only temper in measure the power that the committee now possesses."

Congressman John Blatnik carried this point further: "The Rules Committee never was intended to be a super, all-seeing, all-knowing independent overseer of the House of Representatives. It is not for the Rules Committee to decide what the House shall consider, but rather the order and the condition in which it shall consider the legislative proposals favorably reported to the House by the various legislative committees."

In all of these debates, the question of freedom of speech, constitutionality, precedents about the rights of minorities, and the danger of majority rule are raised. There are frequent appeals to history and to the views of members of Congress and commentators of the past. There are discussions of technicalities and rules of the Senate and of the House of Representatives.

A legislative body, of course, must honor free speech and make adequate provision so that each member individually—speaking for his own constituency or for minorities—can fully present his views and the viewpoint of those whom he represents. Freedom of expression in the Congress is given special protection in the constitutional provision that "for any Speech or Debate in either House, they [the members of Congress] shall not be questioned in any other Place."

Free speech and the right to express minority positions is not the same as unlimited speech. The right to speak fully and without limit of time must be balanced against the right of others to hear the case and their need to hear it before taking action. There rests upon the members of Congress a duty to listen until the point of view of the opposition has been heard. The fulfillment of this duty is not encouraged by unlimited debate.

A legislative assembly is not primarily a debating forum, nor a platform for diverse opinions. It is primarily a law-making body—a place for discussion and the weighing of legislative proposals; a place in which adjustments and amendments in the light of debate, criticisms, and political needs and pressures are worked out. But the final object is to take necessary action that the will of the majority may be expressed, not to the end that government may be conducted for that majority as an end in itself, but rather that it may be conducted for the general good according to the determination of the majority.

In dealing with both of these questions of rules in the Senate and of the Rules Committee in the House, it is important to note that the changes proposed are in rules and procedures rather than in substantive legislation. The action taken is not binding on any citizen, does not give direction to any other institution of government, but relates to Senators and members of the House of Representatives and their conduct of the duties of those two bodies. These are not directly civil rights issues and do not relate to programs for the benefit of one region of the country or one political party or segment of the economy or any of the various definable minority groups in the United States. This is not to imply that procedural rules are not important; on the contrary, the protection of substantive rights and programs depends heavily upon procedures.

Rule by the majority is the basic principle of democracy. This principle is frustrated by conservatives by their continuous opposition to changing the rules of the Senate, by their recourse to these rules in order to prevent majority action in the Senate, and by the continued perennial opposition of the conservatives in the House of Representatives to making the Rules Committee what it properly should be: An instrument by which the majority can properly present its case for action.

Part IV

Liberal vs. Conservative:
Case Histories

☆☆☆ *Chapter 1*
SOCIAL SECURITY:
"TO ENSLAVE WORKERS"

The social security program was initiated in 1935. Today, some 28 years after the enactment of the original Social Security Act, the Old Age, Survivors', and Disability Insurance program is well established as the basic program for assuring some income to individuals and to families who suffer loss of earnings because of the retirement, disability, or death of the worker. The program has become so well accepted that it is somewhat difficult to remember that a little over a quarter of a century ago, when it was first proposed, there were many people who doubted whether it was economically possible or socially desirable or whether it could be made to work at all.

Today nearly 90 percent of all employed workers in this country are in jobs which are covered or are eligible for coverage under the program, in contrast with about 60 percent who were covered when the program was initiated. More than 72 percent of all Americans age 65 or over either are drawing Old Age and Survivors' Insurance benefits or will be eligible to draw them when the worker retires. In 1940 only 8 percent of all Americans over 65 were eligible for such benefits.

The original Social Security Act covered only employees working in industry and commerce. In the last 25 years coverage has been extended to workers in nearly all kinds of employment, and also to the self-employed, including those who work on farms and in private households, in government, and in private nonprofit organizations. Legisla-

95

tion passed in 1956 brought members of the uniformed services into the program on a contributory basis.

Most of the coverage, of course, is compulsory. Problems involving constitutional questions of taxation of state and local governments and the traditionally tax-exempt status of nonprofit organizations have been met by providing for elective coverage. Generally speaking, coverage is available to most such employees on a group-elective basis.

By 1963 the number of Old Age, Survivors', and Disability Insurance beneficiaries had climbed to more than 18 million, a gain of better than 50 percent in the preceding five years. More than 14.4 million of these were old age recipients, and more than 3 million were widowed mothers and children. As of March 1963 there were 768,000 receiving disabled worker benefits.

To indicate the scope of the social security program, statistics show that by the end of 1962 a total of nearly 143 million account numbers had been issued. Some 111 million of the 113 million living persons with accounts had social security earnings credits of one sort or another, and approximately 89.3 million were actually insured. Some 75 million persons paid employment contributions to the social security system at some point in the 1962 year.

Over the years a series of amendments have kept benefits payable under the program reasonably in line with changing economic conditions. By 1950 the average annual earnings of all workers covered under the program had increased 126 percent above 1940 levels, whereas the cost of living had advanced 72 percent. The 1950 amendments provided for the first general increase, raising benefits about 81 percent on the average.

Between 1950 and 1954 the consumer price index rose 12 percent, and the average earnings of workers covered rose about 22 percent. During the same period benefits for those on the social security rolls were increased an average of 15 percent, under the social security amendments of 1952, and by 13 percent under the 1954 amendments. By 1958 the benefits of those who had been on the rolls since the 1954 amendments were found to have fallen behind increases in wage levels by 12 percent and behind increases in the cost of living by 8 percent. The 1958 amendments provided an average 7 percent increase in benefits for both current and future beneficiaries, beginning in January 1959.

Since 1939 the wage base upon which the social security tax is imposed has been enlarged. The original maximum of $3,000 was increased several times: to $3,600 in 1951, to $4,200 in 1955, and to $4,800 beginning in 1959.

In much the same way as the retirement program matured, so has the disability insurance program matured. In the coming years it is expected that the disability program will play an increasingly significant role in meeting the needs of the nation's disabled. The number of workers who meet the direct requirements for protection against loss of earnings through disability is increasing by approximately 2 million a year. At the end of 1964 the number benefiting from the program will have grown to about 1½ million—twice as many as at the end of 1959. This number will continue to rise sharply in the following years, so that eventually the great majority of workers who suffer from long-term critical disabilities will benefit from the protection of the program.

This program was violently opposed by conservatives when it was first presented, and it has been fought by them at nearly every stage at which significant improvement or extension has been proposed.

When the social security program was first proposed, spokesmen for organized business, and conservative members of Congress, attacked it vigorously. They argued that social security would bring about the collapse of capitalism and the American system of government. It would lead to socialism, to government control of industry and the lives of citizens. It would, said James L. Donnelly of the Illinois Manufacturers' Association, destroy initiative, discourage thrift and stifle individual responsibility. Unemployment insurance would relieve people of the necessity to make a living; old age and survivors' insurance would relieve them of the necessity of saving money for retirement. Furthermore, some questioned whether the system could operate on a sound financial basis.

Some of the most outspoken members of the House of Representatives were Republicans from the state of New York. They were disturbed not only by the economic aspects —the payroll tax and the government's role—but about a proposed requirement that wage earners be fingerprinted.

New York Congressman Daniel Reed warned: "Then the lash of the dictator will be felt, and 25 million free American citizens will for the first time submit themselves to a fingerprint test and have their fingerprints filed down here with those of Al Capone and every jailbird and racketeer in the country. That is what it means, and it means that no man can go to an employer and get a job until he goes there with a card issued by the Bureau and can answer the questions and prove that he has been fingerprinted; and if he is not, and they employ him, he is subject to a fine of

$1,000 or 5 years imprisonment, or both. That is what you are trying to do in this bill, and it is in harmony with the dictatorship program launched under the New Deal and to be carried on by it. It is carrying out a program of Karl Marx from beginning to end, the domination of the citizen and the destruction of private industry. This is only one more effort under a dictatorial program to regiment labor and make them submit themselves to this federal test before wage earners can go to an employer and get a job to earn their daily bread.

"I was taught and the people I have the honor to represent believe that the greatest heritage of a free people is the right to transmit that freedom to their children. I loathe this attempt to deceive and betray industry and labor and further fasten upon them this foreign system of regimentation. I shall not—I will not—vote for this bill if title II and title VIII remain in this measure."

Later in the debate, fellow New York Stater John Taber chimed in: "Mr. Chairman, I am not surprised that the members of the Ways and Means Committee on the majority side have not replied to the charge made by the gentleman from New York [Mr. Reed], that this bill was designed to fingerprint and enslave every worker of this land. Never in the history of the world has any measure been brought in here so insidiously designed as to prevent business recovery, to enslave workers, and to prevent any possibility of the employers providing work for the people."

And a third New York Republican Congressman, James W. Wadsworth, stated: "This bill opens the door and invites the entrance into the political field of a power so vast, so powerful as to threaten the integrity of our institutions and to pull the pillars of the temple down upon the heads of our descendants. . . ."

The record of 28 years is a solid historical repudiation of these arguments.

☆☆☆ *Chapter 2*
FDIC: "SUBVERSIVE TO SOUND ECONOMICS"

The Banking Act of 1933 created the Federal Deposit Insurance Corporation. In the original act there were two separate plans for deposit insurance: a temporary one which was intended to be in effect for six months following January

1, 1934, and a permanent one to begin on July 1, 1934. The temporary one was extended twice by the Congress, and the permanent plan—with some changes—was enacted into law in August 1935.

The original deposit insurance law provided that all banks licensed to go back into operation after the banking holiday of 1933 which were also members of the Federal Reserve System had to be insured under the temporary plan. Any nonmember bank certified by a proper state authority to be in solvent condition could also become insured if examined and approved by the Federal Deposit Insurance Corporation. Each bank insured under the temporary plan was assessed one-half of one percent of its deposits which were eligible for insurance, and was subject to a second assessment of equal amount if needed by the Corporation. One-half of the initial assessment was to be paid at once and the rest was payable upon call. The latter was never needed or collected.

The insurance liability was limited in the beginning to $2,500 for each depositor. Capital for the FDIC was provided by the United States Treasury and the 12 Federal Reserve banks. The subscription by the Treasury amounted to $150 million and that of the Federal Reserve banks amounted to one-half of their surplus on January 1, 1933—a total amount of $139 million. Management of the Corporation was placed in the hands of a board of directors consisting of three members, one the Comptroller of the Currency and the other two appointed by the President, with the advice and consent of the Senate, for six-year terms.

In 1934 the coverage was increased from $2,500 to $5,000 for each depositor, and the life of the temporary plan was extended for another year. The Banking Act of 1935 established a permanent program of insurance. It differed considerably from the earlier plan, but was consistent with the purposes of the original act.

The Act has been modified by subsequent legislation, particularly in 1947 and again in 1950.

At the end of 1962 more than 13,000 banks were insured by the Federal Deposit Insurance Corporation, and at the end of that year there were only 368 incorporated banks of deposit in the country that were not insured. One hundred eighty-one of the 368 were mutual savings banks, and of that 181, 173 were insured in the Massachusetts Savings Central Fund Incorporated.

The Corporation insures deposits up to $10,000 for each depositor. Over 98 percent of all deposit accounts in insured banks are fully protected by insurance. A recent study by the FDIC indicates that the present insurance limitation of $10,000 for each depositor could be raised to $25,000 without weakening the insurance fund or increasing bank assessments.

Since its establishment, the Corporation has disbursed approximately $360 million in meeting the demands of 445 insured banks which were in financial trouble; 390 out of the 445 had difficulties in the years from 1934 to 1942, a time when the banking business was working itself out of the depression period. Since 1943 the number of insured banks requiring payment from the Corporation has never exceeded five in any one year.

Estimated recoveries from the disbursements through 1962 amounted to $329.2 million, which would leave an indicated cost of $30.5 million over the period during which it has been in operation.

In December 1962 the assets of the Corporation totaled $2,645 million and its liabilities $43.5 million. This is an excellent record by any standards. Yet when the federal deposit insurance program was first considered, it was subject to the most extreme attack. It was bitterly fought by politicians, businessmen, and bankers.

Mr. U. V. Wilcox, writing in *The American Mercury* (September, 1936) in an article which he entitled "The Bank Insurance Myth," described the Federal Deposit Insurance Corporaton as "the heaviest siege gun adopted up to that date by the New Deal Stormtroopers. It was," he said, "aimed at the money-changers in the Roosevelt temple of purity; and at its breech-end, lanyard in hand, stood a staff of the most noisy and magnificent generals of the More Abundant Life. What they proposed to do appeared gallant in the extreme. The first salvo was to notify the American wage-earner that henceforth and forever, his bank money was insured by the federal government against loss, spoilage, or sudden death; that his savings book was therefore safe and inviolate; that there would never again occur vast losses through mass-closure of banks; and that the financial future of the Republic was to be everlastingly rosy. In other words, the bankers—those 'creatures of entrenched greed'—were to be soundly shelled in their dugouts.

"What issued from that frowning muzzle, however, was not a barrage of shrapnel and high explosive—but a dud. For, sad to relate, the theory of federal bank deposit guarantees has proved itself to be economically unsound and impossible of large-scale application. The promised guarantee is only partial, and is paid for in the main by banks which do not profit from its provisions. The whole scheme has sub-

100

stituted reliance on federal mechanisms for individual brains and corporate responsibility; its only tangible substance is the hold it exercises on the management of banking. In brief, its development has resulted in a financial dictatorship which uses political tools and the mandatory voice of a *Fuhrer* to harass bankers and embarrass depositors. The conclusion to be drawn is extremely obvious—the new rules and regulations are not guarantees of financial security; rather, they are being used as a means by which the Roosevelt bureaucracy hopes to seize absolute control of the banks as one further and important step toward the creation of the New Deal totalitarian state."

It is interesting to note that the bank insurance program was, in fact, not a Roosevelt proposal. It was, perhaps, the only piece of legislation during the famous "First 100 Days" of the New Deal which was neither requested nor supported by the new administration. It was a Congressional proposal; and it was not altogether new. For some 50 years members of Congress had been proposing legislation designed to stabilize the banking industry in the country. A number of individual states had been experimenting with bank obligations insurance for more than a century. The first attempts in the Congress were made in 1886, when a Wisconsin representative introduced a deposit insurance bill in the House. This was followed by similar bills through the years before the turn of the century. None was enacted into law.

In the meantime, deposit insurance on a statewide basis was being debated and was, in fact, adopted in some states. Oklahoma took such action in 1907, and within ten years seven other states—Kansas, Nebraska, Texas, Mississippi, South Dakota, North Dakota, and Washington—adopted similar legislation. Most of these state systems operated successfully for a number of years, but eventually were seriously affected by the agricultural depression of the 1920's. By 1933, for one reason or another every state system had become insolvent.

Whereas emphasis has been placed on the insurance of deposit consequence of the FDIC program, of equal, if not primary, importance was the objective of protecting the circulating medium—that is, money and credit—from the consequences of bank failure. This point has been recognized by the Board of Governors of the Federal Reserve System: "Deposit insurance is potentially one of the more important reforms directed to greater monetary stability by the banking legislation of the 1930's. In essence, these banking reforms aimed at preventing a repetition of the wholesale destruction of the money supply that occurred during 1929-

33. . . . . From the individuals' standpoint, deposit insurance provides protection, within limits, against the banking hazards of deposit ownership. But the major virtue of deposit insurance is for the Nation as a whole. By assuring the public, individuals and businesses alike, that cash in the form of bank deposits is insured up to a prescribed maximum, a major cause of instability in the Nation's money supply is removed." (Federal Reserve Bulletin, February 1950)

The reaction to the proposal for bank insurance was typical of conservative reaction to almost any new proposal. The American Bankers Association passed a resolution asking the President to postpone putting into effect the guarantee of bank deposits. Its objection was twofold; first, the guarantee of deposits was not "sound banking"; and second, there was too little time to make the necessary examination of banks before granting the guarantee. They argued further that guaranteeing deposits would take away the incentive to careful banking.

The Saturday Evening Post of December 23, 1933 carried an editorial entitled "Temporary Expedients." The editorial concluded with these words: "We cannot see any good reasons for a permanent guaranty or for unlimited assessments upon banks which remain open. The temporary plan, in some modified form, would meet every emergency need, and longer-range needs can be met in only one way—by a fundamental reorganization of the banking system. Guaranty is plainly not the ultimate answer, and the sooner that fact is realized the better."

In January 1933, *Nation's Business* magazine, published by the U.S. Chamber of Commerce, carried an article by Francis H. Sisson, president of the American Bankers Association, in which he said:

"There is nothing in our experience with governmental activities in business to warrant the assumption that the extension of government activities in banking would mean greater efficiency and safety. The much discussed proposal to guarantee deposits, for instance, would simply put a premium on bad banking and an unjust burden upon good banking. The trial of this plan of protection in various states has been a conspicuous failure. There is no quality inherent in human beings appointed or elected to government positions that is not inherent in private individuals. . . .

"There can be no legislative substitute for honesty and efficiency in bank management, nor can

102

there be any adequate legislative provision against the destruction wrought by business recessions. Such changes as are necessary to improve banking practice should come through the lessons of experience and economic necessity, without the aid of academic or political correctives.

". . . What American banking needs most is the abolishment of special laws placing it under public regulation and supervision, rather than more statutes for its restriction and control such as have been proposed as a result of the depression."

Similar views, of course, were expressed in the Congress by conservative representatives. One of the most extreme was that of Representative James Robert Claiborne of Missouri, who said on the floor of the House on May 23, 1933:

"If we are to pass this bill, we might just as well take down the statues of Benjamin Franklin throughout the country. We might just as well tell the youth of the country to cease saving. We might just as well tell the strong to load on their backs the weak and carry them, because this act seeks to penalize those banks which in the last few years have practiced sound banking and come through, in favor of those that did not, and who are now suffering. . . ."

Representative Claiborne went on to quote from the American Bankers Association resolution:

"The American Bankers Association has long been opposed to the compulsory guaranty of bank deposits in any form, and is on record by the following resolution setting forth its position on this subject:

"*Resolved*, That the American Bankers Association is unalterably opposed to any plan looking to the mutual guaranty of deposits either by a State or the Nation for the following reasons:

"1. It is a function outside of State or National Government.

"2 It is unsound in principle.

"3. It is impractical and misleading.

"4. It is revolutionary in character.

"5. It is subversive to sound economics.

"6. It will lower the standard of our present banking system.

"7. It is productive of and encourages bad banking.

"8. It is a delusion that a tax upon the strong will prevent failures of the weak.

"9. It discredits honesty, ability and conservation.

"10. A loss suffered by one bank jeopardizes all banks.

"11. The public must eventually pay the tax.

"12. It will cause and not avert panics.

"Resolved, That the American Bankers Association is unalterably opposed to any plan looking to the mutual guaranty of deposits either by a State or the Nation, believing it to be impractical, unsound, misleading, revolutionary in character, and subversive to sound economics, placing a tool in the hands of the unscrupulous and inexperienced for reckless banking, and knowing further that such a law would weaken our banking system and jeopardize the interest of the people."

Whereas full credit for stability in the banking system of the United States cannot be given to the Federal Deposit Insurance Corporation, it undoubtedly has made a great contribution. The record supports what then Representative Lister Hill of Alabama had to say at the close of the debate on this issue in the 73rd Congress: "The country has had nothing comparable to it since the passage of the Federal Reserve Act. It is one of the great pieces of legislation in the history of the government. It is indeed 'the shadow of a great rock in a weary land.' "

Again experience has proved the inadequacy of the conservative judgment and demonstrated the need for the application of reasoned judgment in developing governmental programs to meet economic and fiscal needs.

Chapter 3

REA: "SOCIALISM AND RUSSIANISM"

The year 1960 marked the 25th anniversary of the establishment of the Rural Electrification Administration. When the REA was brought into existence by an executive order signed by President Roosevelt on May 11, 1935, only 10 percent of the farms in America had the benefits of electricity. In many areas electricity was not available to farmers at all, excepting as it might be provided by individually owned gasoline generators or by the even more uncertain source of wind-driven devices for producing electricity.

Twenty-five years later over 96 percent of the farms in the United States not only had electric power available, but were using it, and more than half of these were served by the REA. About 4.7 million consumers, farmers, rural families, schools, churches, and other establishments were being supplied with electricity by approximately 950 local REA cooperatives throughout the nation.

Today, REA has been accepted. It has, at least in the public mind, become respectable. It is no longer believed to be the daring economic and social venture that it was once said to be. It is no longer under frontal attack by its enemies. Its critics hesitate to call it socialism. It has answered the charge that there were no customers willing to buy electric power in rural America. It has proved that farmers as well as people in the cities and the towns enjoy the comforts and convenience of readily available power, light, and heat.

REA loans have proven to be fiscally sound. From the beginning of the new program to January 1, 1963, the REA advanced about $4 billion to REA borrowers on approved loans. In the same period REA borrowers repaid the government about $1.7 billion on their loans. This included $967 million repaid on the principal, $203 million paid ahead of schedule, and $562 million paid in interest.

REA has created a tremendous and vigorous new market supplied in large part by private power companies. It has proved beyond doubt that the availability of electricity for power, light, and heat has greatly increased the productivity of rural America, and thus has stimulated the whole economy of the United States.

Electric sales of REA borrowers totaled about 32 billion kilowatt hours in 1962, and it is estimated that consumers served by the rural electric systems buy $1 billion worth of appliances and equipment each year. REA studies have shown that for every dollar the rural electric cooperative spends in building lines to serve rural families, the average rural consumer spends about four dollars for wiring, plumbing, and electrical appliances and equipment.

The REA was established at a time which was not favorable to its successful growth or development. The country was in the midst of a great depression which affected the people in cities and towns and, in a very special and severe way, people living on the farms of America.

When REA legislation was proposed in 1936, it was subject to all manner of attack. The reaction to this plan to bring electricity to the farms of America serves to some extent to illustrate the contrasting reactions of conservatives and liberals to a problem. One conservative Congressman cried, "It's socialism and Russianism on a giant scale." Another labeled it a "socialistic proposal" and said it would cost the federal Treasury more than a billion dollars. Senator King of Utah raised the usual constitutional question, stating that:

> "In my opinion, there is no constitutional warrant for the measure under consideration. . . .
>
> "What provision of the Constitution warrants or justifies a measure imposing a tax of a billion dollars, as the bill before us originally provided, upon the people of the United States to build electric-light plants, construct transmission lines, and supply individuals with refrigerators and plumbing facilities, electric wiring, and electrical appliances for their homes? These activities belong to the realm of individual and private enterprise. . . .
>
> ". . . If the Federal Government is without authority to enact a measure to furnish electricity to a limited number of agriculturalists and to supply them with electrical appliances, refrigerators, plumbing, and so forth, then it would be an invalid act to impose taxes upon the American people for that purpose. . . .
>
> ". . . How can it be said that the furnishing of electricity to farmers in rural communities is for the general welfare of the United States? This

106

is clearly a local matter and not a matter of national concern. . . ."

The constitutional argument of Senator King was supported by Representative Schuyler Merritt of Connecticut, who said:

"I do not think to help these citizens we ought to endanger the structure of our Government, which I think we are doing by putting the Federal Government into all sorts of things that the States ought to attend to themselves. You must bear in mind that where our States are more fully electrified today, this has been done without any help from the Federal Government. . . .

"I think it is not possible for these emergency Federal organizations to become permanent without producing in this country a bureaucratic and socialistic state; and all these autocratic bureaus will finally merge and come under control of an individual autocrat. The history of all nations shows that a bureaucratic state must end in a dictatorship. I hope and believe that our country is more concerned in maintaining the freedom and enterprise of its constituent States and of all our citizens than in endeavoring by unconstitutional means to help a certain class who can and will be helped by other means."

The charge of politics was raised. It was argued that REA was unnecessary, that we had at that time a surplus of power. The obvious point was made that several private power companies had surplus generating capacity, running as high as a billion kilowatts, without customers.

Representative James Wadsworth supported this position in an argument made in April of 1936: "My judgment is that this bill, if passed, will not only bring disappointment with respect to the frequency with which its provisions are taken advantage of but it will also bring disappointment with respect to the number of local companies that the Government will have to take over, because they will be carrying a debt equal to 100 percent of their assets."

This position was also that of the private utilities, as presented in an article by H. S. Bennion of the Edison Electrical Institute:

"In farm electrification, as in other fields of electrical development, the electric light and power companies in the United States have been the pioneers and leaders in extending electric lines into farm territory and in developing equipment, methods, and uses for making electricity profitable as well as convenient for the farmers. . . .

"It has as yet been uneconomic to extend electric service to the great majority of farms in the United States. This will continue to be the situation for many years to come. The cost of building lines to reach these farms is out of all proportion to the benefits to be derived by the farmer from the use of electricity. Considering the obstacles and the economic problems to be met, however, the electric-light and power companies of America over the past fifteen years have made remarkable progress in carrying electricity to the farm, much more progress than any other country has made. . . ."

It was generally agreed that REA organizations or farm groups could not effectively carry out the intentions of the Act. Mr. Hudson W. Reed, management engineer with the United Gas Improvement Company of Philadelphia, said:

"It may again take some time for it to be realized that inexperienced and poorly organized farm groups cannot hope to operate as cheaply and efficiently as well-trained and highly specialized utility organizations. . . .

"The history of Government operation or sponsorship of such projects (as REA) here and elsewhere, indicates that over and over again the taxpayers have had to pay the losses incurred. There is nothing in the present plan to indicate that history will not again repeat itself."

Opponents of REA attacked with deeds as well as words, using a variety of means to discourage the development of REA-supported rural cooperatives.

"Spite lines" were a frequent technique. When a private utility learned that a cooperative was being organized to provide rural electric service, the utility would quickly run a line of its own through the more thickly populated part of the proposed service area, "skimming the cream" of the customers by taking those who could be served at least cost. Other potential customers in the thinly populated parts of the area were left without access—and the cost of serving them separately would usually be too high to justify an REA loan.

Another technique reportedly used by the private utilities was to wait till a cooperative set out stakes for a line, and then quickly to set up private-line poles along the same route and to claim that the cooperative was going to duplicate an existing private line.

Then there were tactics aimed at the farmers themselves: propaganda in newspaper advertisements and articles and by word of mouth, warning prospective cooperative customers that their REA-sponsored service would be inadequate or that signing up for an REA cooperative would mean mortgaging their property.

Harry Slattery in *Rural America Lights Up* cites farmers' affidavits relating to the attempt of the Alabama Power Company to break up a cooperative project in Cherokee County:

Farmer E. A. Higgins: "An employee of the Alabama Power Company informed me that to sign up for service and take service from the cooperative would be the same as signing a mortgage on my farm. That it would be the same as signing a joint note for the cost of constructing the system, that I would be individually liable for the construction cost of the system and for any damage that might arise out of the construction or operation of the system, that if lightning should strike a line knocking it down and it should kill a mule or do other damage that I would be responsible therefor."

Farmer G. L. Grant: "He (company agent) insists that I'm not using good judgment by waiting until the corporation (the cooperative) brings power to me, as I live so far from the source of power that the power will be so weak that it will not make a light bulb grow red."

The private utilities sent men through a proposed cooperative's area to encourage opposition to the cooperative and to try by personal persuasion to discourage membership.

Again, when a cooperative distributing system tried to buy wholesale power from a private utility's generating plant, the private company, in some cases, would ask high charges for the power.

Or when a cooperative had been organized and had received its REA loan allotment, the private utilities—using influence where required—would offer to buy out the cooperative. In some cases they succeeded.

Then there were assorted legal actions to challenge or at least delay REA cooperatives in their electrification projects. Some questioned the legality of cooperatives under state statutes, while others were harassments—demands for hearings or injunctions. While these legal delays were being employed, the private utilities would keep telling the farmers that the cooperative lines would never be strung.

Despite this opposition the REA was established by the President in 1935, and in the following year was formally approved by the Congress in the passage of the Rayburn-Norris Act.

The principal effort to undercut REA in recent years has been along the lines of weakening its financial structure by limiting its funds and by raising the interest rates on REA borrowing. In some instances this has taken the form of attempting to eliminate the loan authorizations; in others, of attempting to change the interest rate from the statutory 2 percent to a higher rate, or to force REA to borrow funds from private financial institutions. In 1959 it was suggested that the rural electrification systems establish their own bank. This was proposed by President Eisenhower in his 1960 budget message.

Extreme statements have been circulated attempting to persuade the American people that cooperatives, including the REA, are escaping large amounts of tax payments.

Misleading advertisements in the leading magazines of the country proclaim to the public that millions of tax dollars are lost each year through special tax treatment given to cooperatives and REA electric associations. The implication is that not only are the cooperatives not paying taxes, but there is something illicit in their escape.

One such statement, widely circulated a few years ago, declared that farmer cooperatives were escaping $200 million a year in federal income taxes. Dr. Joseph Knapp, Administrator of the Farmers' Cooperative Service, has testified before a Congressional committee that all farmer cooperatives now pay federal income tax at corporation rates on any net margin of operating receipts over expenditures that they retain and treat as their own.

Senator George Aiken of Vermont asked Dr. Knapp how much the total amount of patronage refunds to members had been in the most recent year for which figures were available. He was told that in 1954 they amounted to $238 million. On hearing this, Senator Aiken commented: "Then what about the charge that cooperatives receive $200 million in tax benefits because of patronage refunds? Cooperatives," he said, "cannot possibly escape $200 million in taxes on $238 million of total refunds."

Somewhat less direct than these attacks are those which water down the effectiveness of public power projects. This

110

was an issue in the Dixon-Yates contract—an attempt to tie unusual costs of power production and the financing thereof into the TVA, and thereby to dilute and weaken TVA and to make it less effective as an operating unit.

The opposition to the development of Hell's Canyon Dam on the Snake River in Idaho bears upon this same problem. It was declared that the dam proposed by the Idaho Power Company would be built at no cost to the taxpayer. The chief accountant of the Federal Power Commission testified, however, that the company's write-off to accelerate depreciation would cost the Treasury $83.5 million. More serious than this was the fact that, according to the Federal Power Commission examiner, the prime power capacity of the three company dams would be 505,000 kilowatts—in comparison with the proposed federal high dam, which would have a prime capacity of 924,000 kilowatts. This is not a case of a "giveaway" but, in effect, of a "throwaway" —a waste of potential electric generating power. Not only is the power lost in cases of this kind, but so are the additional benefits of irrigation, flood control—and, in some cases, navigation and recreational facilities.

Many of these arguments against REA seem plausible on their face, but they do not take into account the fact that REA associations are different from other power companies in several respects and do meet special needs. They are 100 percent debt-financed, and even with federally insured mortgages they would be acceptable clients in the money market only at exorbitant interest rates. Doubling the interest rates paid by REA would greatly increase the cost of operation, since interest rates are such a substantial part of the operating cost of a debt-financed utility. (More than 8 percent of the operating revenue of REA borrowers in calendar year 1958 was paid out in interest on their long-term debts.)

One of the principal arguments for the terms extended to REA borrowers derives from the specific responsibilities and likewise the specific restrictions placed on REA borrowers by the Congress. These put REA cooperatives in a different category from other utilities:

1) REA loan funds cannot be used to serve any consumers who already have central-station electricity.

2) As a general rule, REA funds cannot be used to serve consumers who live in a town of more than 1,500 population.

3) In the Pace Act of 1944, the Congress set the interest rate at a flat 2 percent, but in return Congress made it clear that it expected the REA borrowers to provide "area coverage"—to serve everyone in their area who wants electricity,

111

even though it may require very expensive construction to service remote farms.

In effect, then, REA's are called upon to serve rural people wherever they are, but they are excluded from most of the premium markets. REA systems average 3.3 consumers per mile of line, while commercial companies, serving the much more heavily populated areas, average 30 or more consumers per mile. In 1960 the more densely settled areas produced annual revenues of $6,580 per mile, in contrast to only $414 per mile for the rural electric systems.

The whole program of the REA cooperatives must be considered in the light of some of the general economic trends in the United States today. First, the rapid growth of large scale—even monopolistic—business and industry, and the corresponding decline in competitive small business, must be taken into account. The second factor is the continuously widening gap between farm income and the economic welfare of the agricultural population on the one hand, and the rest of the economy on the other.

Total net farm income declined from $14 billion in 1950 to $11.6 billion in 1956, and then managed to reach $13 billion in 1961. At the same time, total national income increased from $241.9 billion in 1950 to $427.8 billion in 1961. Failures of small independent businesses have multiplied at the same time as economic power has been more and more concentrated in the hands of a few large businesses and industries.

In view of these facts, the liberal position is that it is of vital importance that the agricultural economy of the country be strengthened. It is also of vital importance that local ownership be encouraged, that local communities be strengthened and revitalized. The continued strength and growth of the REA cooperative will contribute to the realization of these two objectives. The cooperatives help to maintain the independence and economic strength of the farmer and of the small businesses which are directly dependent upon him.

Certainly, it has been a good thing for America to have several million farmers and rural families join together to bring electricity to the farms and small communities of rural America—especially when it had not been done, and very likely would not otherwise have been done.

All of this is fundamental to preserving and strengthening the economic freedom of America, and, with that freedom as a basis, to strengthening all of the other great freedoms so essential to the leading of a good and full and responsible life.

There remains a tremendous unfilled need for more and

cheaper power in the United States. Not all this power need be supplied through REA distribution systems or REA generating plants. It is a problem for the Rural Electrification Administration, for the private utilities, for the Bureau of Reclamation, and for other governmental and nongovernmental institutions that may be involved in this common effort.

☆☆☆ *Chapter 4*
TVA: "THE MUDHOLES OF TENNESSEE"

This year (1963) the Tennessee Valley Authority is 30 years old. The Tennessee Valley system now consists of a series of 31 dams, 25 of which were built and acquired by the TVA and six of which are privately owned. Six of these are in the Cumberland River Valley but are related to the Tennessee Valley Authority project.

The flood control operation of TVA has proved itself able to stop the flow of the Tennessee River—as it did in 1958, 1960 and 1961—and to control flooding on the lower Ohio and down the Mississippi. Navigation on the Tennessee River has improved to the point where the river now provides a commercial water channel of some 650 miles, from Knoxville, Tennessee to Paducah, Kentucky. In 1961 commercial tonnage on the channel totaled approximately 12 million tons.

In addition to these major achievements, the Tennessee Valley Authority has been most effective and most useful in providing electric power. In 1933 there were only 300,000 power consumers in the whole Tennessee Valley; today there are more than 1.5 million. In 1933 the average consumer used 600 kilowatts of electric power, while today the average kilowatt consumption per consumer is over 9,500. This is twice the national average.

The whole face of the valley has changed as a result of TVA production of inexpensive electric power. Ninety-eight percent of all the farms of the valley have electricity. During World War II, approximately 75 percent of TVA output went into war production to help meet the nation's need for copper, aluminum, synthetic rubber, and other necessary minerals and chemicals. The existence of TVA power was one of the reasons for the establishment of the Oak Ridge atomic research program in Tennessee. Even today the

Atomic Energy Commission and other governmental agencies use approximately one-half of all the power generated by the Tennessee Valley Authority.

In the valley itself, of course, there is no serious criticism of or opposition to the agency. It is regularly endorsed by candidates of both parties in national elections. In his 1960 campaign, President Kennedy, speaking in Nashville, said that "the Tennessee Valley is the greatest asset we could have, not just to the Tennessee Valley, and not just to the United States, but to all those people who stand today in the underdeveloped world and try to make a judgment which road they will take."

TVA has not always been popular. At its beginning it was violently opposed. *Time* magazine, in a recent issue, quoted a speech made in the Congress in 1933 by Rhode Island's Senator Jesse Houghton Metcalf, who, speaking shortly after the Congress had acted to reduce veterans' benefits, raised this question: "How on earth can we justify taking a decent living from the soldiers who suffered on the battlefields of France and pour it into the mudholes of Tennessee?"

Wendell Willkie, testifying in 1933 before the House Military Affairs Committee, as president of the Commonwealth and Southern Corporation, opposed a fully effective Tennessee Valley Authority and made some rather extreme predictions.

"I want to say, Mr. Chairman," he commented, "that no one has read or referred with more gratification than we have of this magnificent proposed development of the Tennessee Valley." He strongly objected, however, to the building of government transmission lines. "To take our market," he told the committee, "is to take our property." Let government make cheap power at Muscle Shoals, Willkie contended, but let it be sold to the utilities and distributed by them through privately owned transmission lines. Unless this change were made, Willkie said that he must oppose the bill. "I can say to you, as my deliberate judgment, that if this bill passes, this $400,000,000 worth of [Commonwealth and Southern] securities will be eventually destroyed."

Willkie contended that the Tennessee Valley, in any case, was "more than adequately served" by the existing Commonwealth and Southern system. There was, he said, an excess generating capacity of 66⅔ percent in the valley. His supporting cast spelled out the argument that the valley was absorbing all the power it could use in the foreseeable future. . . ." (*The Coming of the New Deal* by Arthur Schlesinger, Jr., pp. 325-6)

In the House of Representatives the bill faced strong opposition, led by Congressman Martin of Massachusetts: "I think," Martin said, "I can accurately predict no one in this generation will see materialize the industrial-empire dream of the Tennessee Valley."

TVA is not popular in all places even today. It is generally opposed by privately owned electric utilities, and by the Chambers of Commerce in most areas of the country—outside the valley itself. It had some of its most difficult years in the Fifties when it was called "creeping socialism" by President Eisenhower and was made a target in the proposed Dixon-Yates contract. As a government project, TVA inevitably will remain subject to some controversy.

It is a fact that TVA has been subsidized. Over the last 30 years, $2 billion in federal funds has been spent by TVA —about half on power facilities and the other half on developmental programs, reforestation, and the like. One billion dollars has been spent on power. It is expected that this will be paid back over the next 50 years. The financing of TVA has been changed so that under existing law the agency must raise funds for its power operations by selling its own bonds. This year (1963) TVA asked the Congress for only $36 million.

The opposition of the coal industry and of the mine workers has largely dissipated, since at the present time two-thirds of the electricity is generated in coal-fired steam plants. The TVA has become the largest user of coal in the United States. Private utilities in the area have not been stifled but have been given an expanded opportunity for both the production and distribution of electricity and for the sale of equipment and supplies that go with the use of power.

The Tennessee Valley Authority was an application of what in some ways was not an original New Deal concept of resources and development. In a message to the Congress in 1908, Theodore Roosevelt said: "Every stream should be used to its utmost. . . . Each river system, from its headwaters in the forest to its mouth on the coast, is a single unit and should be treated as such."

President Franklin Roosevelt in 1933 asked the Congress to establish an agency which would be "a corporation clothed with the power of government but possessed with the flexibility and initiative of private enterprise." The Authority was given the responsibility for comprehensive development of the resources of the seven states in the Tennessee Valley area.

TVA has proved itself, but beyond that, it has proved

115

that there is a place for government action in conditions and circumstances in which private enterprise or individual effort may be inadequate or too slow. The Tennessee Valley Authority is an example of government doing for an area of the country what the people of the area could not do themselves.

Part V

MIXING IN THE MODERN WORLD

☆☆☆ *Chapter 1*
THE TRIBULATIONS OF TRADE

Apart from a few extreme protectionists, there was no real opposition to the most recent action to liberalize trade policy in the Trade Expansion Act of 1962. There were scattered demands for protection of particular industries, but the general idea of free trade was in no way seriously challenged. Liberals continued their traditional support and conservative spokesmen for big business in the United States were among its strongest and most outspoken advocates.

To be sure, there were demands that the escape clause provisions in present trade laws be strengthened, and that quotas be used as an instrument for the protection of American industry and American jobs. Some recognition was given to these demands in the drafting of the Trade Act. For the most part, however, the thrust of the legislation was toward the elimination of existing trade barriers and the encouragement of free trade among the nations of the world. Liberalization of tariffs and trade policy is not an answer to all the difficulties in international exchange today; it does, however, establish a standard against which restrictive practices and programs may be judged, and also an objective toward which all nations may work.

In the international economic picture there have been three developments of major significance: first, the rapid economic and industrial growth of Western Europe and the establishment of the Common Market; second, the continuing and in some cases intensified economic competition of the Soviet

117

bloc; and third, the emerging demands of both old and new underdeveloped countries for better treatment in world markets and in some cases for a larger share of traditional markets.

Competitive advantages once held by the United States have been greatly reduced. The advantage we had of being able to obtain money for investment at lower interest rates has been significantly reduced as political stability and economic strength have returned to Western Europe. With the opening up of world supplies of raw materials, the edge the United States once held by way of easy access to raw materials has also been reduced. The technological gap, too, has been narrowed through the rebuilding of Western Europe and Japan and through the construction of new factories with the most advanced equipment in other parts of the world.

With the establishment of the Common Market and, beyond that, the growing ease of access to world markets, the advantage which we held as the result of having a large and unified national market for our mass-produced products is not as significant as it once was. In international competition our chief advantages today are in the control of capital, in special technical knowledge and skills, in our great reservoir of managerial ability, and in our greater stability, both economic and political.

These advantages, however, do not permit us to operate at will in international trade and commerce. The United States must take into account international developments and realities. Whereas the very early actions taken by the Common Market have been on the side of protection and restrictive trade, our continuing hope and confidence is that this is temporary, and that once relations within the market itself have been reasonably stabilized, the impetus will be toward the removal of trade barriers between the Common Market and the rest of the free world. The additional or higher tariffs which have been imposed during the early months of the existence of the market have, of course, been disturbing, especially to the industries directly affected. However, in terms of the total volume of trade between the Common Market and the rest of the free world, their quantitative significance is very limited.

The matter of competition from the Soviet bloc raises questions which are in part economic and in part political. There are really two problems: one, that of competition of Soviet goods with American or free world products in those markets which are open to the products of both; and two, that of trade between our allies (or, in some cases, our own

118

country) and the Soviets or members of the Communist bloc.

The Communist bloc continues to utilize economic assistance along with military assistance in seeking to advance its aims in the less-developed countries. The Sino-Soviet aid program averaged about $1 billion annually over the 1959-61 period, and although there has been a reduction in new economic aid commitments over the last year or so, the implementation of the existing agreements has increased significantly. The amount of new credit extended in 1962 was about $520 million.

The decline in aid corresponds with reports of mounting problems in the use of resources and in production in the Soviet Union and throughout the Soviet bloc. It may also reflect a political decision to cut back new commitments for the time being, since the difference between commitments and the actual performance is of such a size as to prove embarrassing to the Soviet Union.

Total credits and grants extended between 1955 and the end of 1962 to some thirty countries outside the Soviet bloc itself totaled more than $5 billion. At the same time it is estimated that about 11,000 economic technicians were employed in less developed countries during the latter half of 1962, an increase of 35 percent over the same period in 1961. The number of military technicians more than doubled. In all of these cases, of course, it is extremely difficult to distinguish between military and nonmilitary technicians.

The credits given by the Communists have been extended primarily for developmental projects. Buildings and equipment for manufacturing purposes account for more than half of these obligations, while multipurpose projects involving such things as reclamation and irrigation, agricultural development, power projects, transportation and communications, surveys and exploration account for most of the rest. At least nine countries have received credit lines in excess of $100 million. These are Afghanistan, Argentina, Ethopia, India, Indonesia, Iraq, Syria, Egypt and Cuba.

The assistance from the U.S.S.R. is rarely in the form of grants. The interest rates are low, typically 2.5 percent, and repayment is usually on the basis of a twelve-year period or longer. When the Communist satellites extend credit they usually do so for a shorter term of five to eight years, and the interest rates ordinarily run about 4 or 5 percent. The pattern is slightly different when Communist China is involved. Its credit tends to carry lower interest rates than does the Soviet credit. It is more inclined to use grants rather than loans. However, the Chinese assistance program

119

is of limited importance because of its small scale. Even the total effort on the part of all the Communist countries does not approach in size the effort we have made, but it has nonetheless been effective.

The Communists operate on a highly selective basis, concentrating on those areas in which it is believed the greatest political gain is possible. There is always a grave question as to whether or not this commitment will be kept. Yugoslavia, for example, learned a lesson when the credits provided by Russia were withdrawn for political reasons.

Because it tends to move in and out of a market in accordance with the political opportunity at hand, the Soviet Union is an irregular trade partner. Many underdeveloped countries, in particular, have experienced feasts and famines at the table of the trade monopoly of the U.S.S.R.

In Burma, for example, the Soviet Union all but passed out of the picture in 1958, after buying millions of dollars worth of rice in 1957. But even as they bought this rice, they were contributing much to the disorder in Burma.

The Soviet Union stopped buying wool from New Zealand in 1959, presumably in order to make a more impressive showing in Australia.

The Soviet Union's economic offensive seeks to disrupt normal commercial cooperation between the industrial nations of the West and the underdeveloped countries which need capital, to snare other nations into becoming economically dependent on the Soviet Union, and to promote friction within the Western alliance.

One of the major causes of friction between the United States and other members of the Western alliance is that of trade and commerce with Russia or with the Soviet bloc. This gives rise to Congressional protests and, in some cases, to far-reaching demands that we impose special commercial sanctions against those who carry on such trade. This point has been raised most recently with reference to commerce with Cuba.

Within recent years Russian agents have succeeded in purchasing such things as modern tire-making installations and complete plants for the production of plastics, such as polyethylene and synthetic fibers. The biggest chemical firms in Britain were involved in these transactions. The Soviet agents have been able to purchase from France an automatic production line for making truck parts, a modern cement factory, and two complete plants for the manufacture of concrete panels used in rapid-method construction. In recent years Germany has shown a willingness to sell the fruits of its most advanced technological processes, and

120

equipment necessary to these processes, to the Russians. Such areas as chemicals, pulp and paper, and tubing mills for the manufacture of oil pipelines were included.

When Mr. Mikoyan was in the United States in 1959 he attempted to negotiate with our government for the purchase of large-scale pipeline equipment. The United States had the capacity to produce the very large tubing which was necessary for the pipelines the Soviet Union wanted to build. However, we rejected the request, and the Soviet representatives immediately went to West Germany, where they negotiated a contract with the sheet metal and tubing companies for the same materials we had refused to supply.

In Italy, too, the Soviet drive to extract technological know-how has been successful. In 1961 the Soviet trade ministry concluded a trade agreement with the Italian government. The agreement provided for the export by five major Italian manufacturing firms—Montecatini, Saicci, Chatillion, ENI, and Projetti—of complete plants and processes. The plants to be supplied by these firms were to include the latest equipment to produce the following commodities: methanol, acetylene, ethylene, maleic anhydridge, ammonia, diamine, paper pulp, pipelines, and remote control equipment.

Oil trade between the U.S. and some of the western nations and the Russians has also caused serious concern, although there have been encouraging indications of change with reference to trade in oil. The Soviet Union has been offering petroleum products in selected markets at 20 to 35 percent below going market prices. In addition, it offers to accept payment in local currency or in local export products. These offers have all the characteristics of an irresistible bargain. They have been carefully designed, in fact, to carry that kind of appeal.

The Italian case is illustrative. In November 1960 a trade agreement was concluded between the two countries whereby Italy would receive, over a five-year period, some 100,000 barrels of Russian oil per day. The unique feature of this deal was the discount price. To make sure that no other supplier could compete for this sale, the Soviet trade monopoly depressed the price to $1 a barrel delivered at a Black Sea port, a figure 37.5 percent below the price at which Middle East oil could be picked up at the nearest port.

If this kind of economic aggression and penetration continues on a large scale, it could cause serious economic harm to Britain—which depends in no small measure upon her capacity to export Middle Eastern oil—and to the free world. In the first place, the price is so low that it cannot be met competitively by the major oil suppliers. (For example, in the case of Kuwait oil, among the cheapest to extract, the oil companies are obliged to pay the Sheik 69.5 cents per barrel in royalties alone, as provided by the 50-50 terms of the contract governing their concession.) In the second place, after the Russian crude oil has been processed in Italy, it enjoys the status of a Common Market product. In the third place, the growing dependence of any member of the NATO community on Russian oil raises all kinds of disquieting prospects for the future, both short and long run.

This action of the Russians dealt a distinct shock to an already saturated market. There was also, in the background, the clear threat of still larger imports from the same source. Unfortunately, too, the Soviet move came just at the time when the first concerted steps had begun to be taken by the Arab oil countries with a view to stabilizing the financial returns from their oil resources.

Both economic and political considerations are important in responding to this kind of challenge. The internal political problems of the nations of the Western world, especially as these problems reflect the economic pressures, do have some bearing upon our decisions on trade policy. So do the particular relationships in other areas of international competition and disagreement bear upon the question of trade with the Soviet Union and with the Soviet bloc.

The same is true with regard to arrangements with the uncommitted nations and with the developing nations, which for the most part are producers either of single crops—or at least of a single export crop—and in most cases do not possess the economic strength or the organizational ability to conduct an orderly marketing program. This is especially true in such things as coffee, sugar, and the like. These difficulties require a very special kind of response which is both political and economic—and, in a way, outside the normal and traditional practices of both international trade and diplomacy.

Coffee and sugar require some kind of international or world agreement, where this is possible without participation of the Soviets. The use of quotas is justified both in terms of the total amount to be admitted and also with reference to the amount that we agree to accept from any one country. This was the practice in the procurement of sugar until 1962, when the traditional practice of assigning shares of our sugar needs to foreign suppliers was modified to the extent of purchasing a significant part of our sugar imports in the world market, at world prices. The recent dislocations in the sugar market are in part traceable to our departure from the

122

established practice of allocating quotas to suppliers, particularly in Central America.

Of all the issues on which there is a liberal-conservative division in the United States, the issue of trade is the one in which the difference is most difficult to establish, or to clarify.

If there is any major discernible difference in the general area of these difficult problems, it is, I think, on this point: Whereas the conservatives tend to cry at one moment for free trade and at another time for rather violent economic reprisals, the liberals are more ready to resort to international agreements or to try a variety of methods and procedures in the hope that some kind of rational control can be exercised and the general good of our own country and our allies may be thereby advanced.

☆☆☆ *Chapter 2*
THE TWO CONSPIRACIES

Reinhold Niebuhr, in a book on politics published in 1960, stated the general case against the conservative position in American foreign policy in recent years when he said: "When one turns to examine the role of conservatism in American foreign policy, the distinctive trait appears to be a curious ambivalence between isolationism and imperialism, between a disavowal of the responsibilities of our power and an exercise of that power without a sense of its limits. . . .

"In one moment," he continued, "it is ready to discount all the perils in which we stand and to counsel the nation to 'cut its losses' lest further involvement in world responsibilities increase our tax rate. In the next moment it is ready to use our economic power to force European nations into free enterprise patterns after our image, however irrelevant these patterns may be to the necessities of the recipient nations, and to employ our economically based military power in Asia in such a way as to make our struggle with communism appear a purely military venture, thus alienating such vast uncommitted Asiatic nations as India. The enormous social convulsions of the continent in travail are such a mystery to this type of mind that even the most catastrophic upheavals are attributed to mistakes made in our State Department."

This was a judgment passed at a time when the extent of

confusion and of contradiction in world affairs was becoming clear and when the general conservative reaction was somewhat more frantic than it is today.

In attempting to distinguish between the liberal and conservative response in the field of foreign policy today, one must judge more by words than by action. On the record, since the end of World War II those who are called conservatives—at least those of that tendency who are in Congress —have generally given support to foreign aid programs and supported our international commitments. There have been some aberrations, as in the relatively strong support for the Bricker amendment, which would have subjected many executive decisions in the field of foreign policy to Congressional review, and which, had it been adopted, would have set almost impossible obstacles in the way of the conduct of foreign policy. This amendment was never acted upon and disappeared from the political scene with the election of a Republican President. There is no indication as yet of its revival, but perhaps too little time has passed.

Criticism of conservatives today is justified at least on the grounds that they have greatly oversimplified foreign problems.

In her book *The Mind of the Maker,* Dorothy Sayres has an essay entitled the "Problem Picture." In the introduction to this essay she quotes these words from the Stevenson Lectures of Mr. L. P. Jacks, given in 1926 and 1927:

> "I am informed by philologists that the 'rise to power' of these two words, 'problem' and 'solution' as the dominating terms of public debate, is an affair of the last two centuries, and especially of the nineteenth, having synchronized, so they say, with a parallel 'rise to power' of the word 'happiness'—for reasons which doubtless exist and would be interesting to discover. . . .
>
> "On the whole, the influence of these words is malign, and becomes increasingly so. They have deluded poor men with Messianic expectations . . . which are fatal to steadfast persistence in good workmanship and to well-doing in general. . . . Let the valiant citizen never be ashamed to confess that he has no 'solution of the social problem' to offer his fellow-men. Let him offer them rather the service of his skill, his vigilance, his fortitude and his probity. For the matter in question is not primarily a problem, nor the answer to it a solution."

For example, Senator Tower submitted a resolution on foreign policy in the 87th Congress which declared, among other things, that the purposes of the United States in its relation with other nations of the world should be: support for all nations subjected to Soviet, Communist Chinese, or other communist control since 1939; the right of free choice of government, after proper preparation and under appropriate electoral supervision; the reduction of communist war machines and the economies which support them to levels at which they can no longer threaten the peace of the world; the support and defense of those whose freedom is threatened.

In a similar vein, Senator Goldwater's book, *The Conscience of a Conservative,* gives what he calls an outline for victory: "Our strategy," he says, "must be primarily offensive in nature . . . we should adopt a discriminating foreign-aid policy . . . we should encourage the captive peoples to revolt against their Communist rulers . . . we must —ourselves—be prepared to undertake military operations against vulnerable Communist regimes. . . ."

In the same book, Senator Goldwater asserts that, "The American government does not have the right, much less the obligation, to try to promote the economic and social welfare of foreign peoples. Of course, all of us are interested in combating poverty and disease wherever it exists. *But the Constitution does not empower our government to undertake that job in foreign countries,* no matter how worthwhile it might be. Therefore, except as it can be shown to promote America's national interests, the Foreign Aid program is unconstitutional."

The Senator goes on to say, ". . . yet every one of the 'neutral' countries we are aiding is committed to a system of State Socialism. Our present policy of government-to-government aid strengthens Socialism in those countries. We are not only perpetuating the inefficiency and waste that always attends government-controlled economies, by strengthening the hand of those governments, we are making it more difficult for free enterprise to take hold. For this reason alone, we should eliminate all government-to-government capital assistance and encourage the substitution of American private investment."

It adds little to the development or the execution of foreign policy to say that such policy must be discriminating; or to say that every one of the neutral countries we are aiding is committed to a system of state socialism, when this is not the fact; or to declare that foreign aid programs are unconstitutional. The fact is that there is a necessity to participate in international society today and such participation raises increasingly difficult problems of the international common good and what often appears to be a conflict between that good and our own proper national interest.

Today the areas of conflict and confusion are many. We are challenged in ways and places which do not permit decisive response. World leadership carries limitations which were not present 25, 50, or 100 years ago. We cannot always impose international policy at will, no matter how right we may be, without taking into account the judgment and even the national interests of other states—our allies or, in some cases, those who are at least not actively aligned against us.

The fact that we live in the same world with a communist power which has declared itself to be our enemy complicates our problems. Coexistence is not our choice, but it is a fact. The problem, therefore, involves the conditions and the terms under which we shall coexist. The condition of this contest and the conduct of what is called the "cold war" raises hard questions, both practical and moral.

We can no longer say, as we once did, that our concern is simply the defense of Western civilization, because we are involved to a greater or lesser degree in common causes with countries that are a part of other civilizations and other cultures. We are no longer merely supporting democratic governments, although we espouse the principle of self-determination, for we work with governments which are in some degree authoritarian and nondemocratic. We cannot draw a hard line with regard to economic systems, insisting that our allies' economies be identical in organization and operation with ours. We accept that there may be some accommodation between private ownership and state and social ownership and control.

The pursuit of national interest alone does not give us a ready answer to every question. Dr. John Bennett, dean of the faculty of Union Theological Seminary, inquired into the bearing of ethics on foreign policy in a speech which he gave in Washington in 1961. He said that he was never satisfied by the way in which people dealt with the question of ethics and national interest; that he had not been able to arrive at an adequate formulation himself.

It is clear that some standards must be applied. Whereas the whole truth need not always be told to everyone, friendly nations do have a right to greater frankness than do enemies. Though we recognize the need for espionage, we do not at the same time say that there are no restraints upon the methods which may be used and the manner in which peo-

126

ple may be exploited. Morality does not stop at the water's edge, nor at the entrance to the CIA or the Pentagon. We have never accepted that national interest can ultimately and completely or in every case override considerations of right or wrong.

Questions of foreign policy cannot be dealt with in terms of simple absolutes. Compromise, obviously, is called for. Compromise may sometimes be unwise, but it is not in itself immoral or treasonable.

Adlai Stevenson has properly described the moral and political framework within which foreign policy decisions must be made: "There are limits to the effectiveness of our nation's foreign policy. For foreign policy is concerned with problems which lie beyond our jurisdiction and about which we cannot legislate. There are only two means available for influencing the actions of other states: persuasion and coercion. As a free society, we must rely primarily on persuasion. We can use coercion only rarely, and usually only as a defensive measure. We cannot have satellites, because this depends on the use of coercion. We cannot employ threats and intimidation effectively because our actions are open to free discussion and criticism. . . ." (*Call to Greatness,* pp. 103-4)

The challenge to the United States is being presented in the form of two conspiracies. One is the formal and clearly identified conspiracy of communism, whose purposes have been stated, whose methods have been defined, whose procedures and actions are already manifest. This is a conspiracy which deserves our attention. It cannot be answered by vague protestations of innocence and of simplicity, or by simply pointing to our record of the past.

The second conspiracy is a conspiracy in the more fundamental meaning of the word: of breathing together, of aspiring together, and of thinking together. This is a conspiracy which demands respect for the dignity of every man. It requires us to be concerned about justice for every man, to acknowledge that there is in process a revolution which is fed by hunger and exploitation and disease, and by a conviction that injustice is not a matter of fate. This is an acknowledgment of what was stated by Charles Pèguy in his essay on *The Rights of Man:* that a declaration of justice is in itself instantaneously a declaration of war or of revolution.

This challenge requires action in two major areas. One is in the field of human rights, and involves the question of the rights of our own people and also those of more than two-thirds of the people of the world who are of other races and cultures. The second is that of economic justice, which in-

127

cludes positive action to stimulate economic growth to meet the needs of our own people, and to undertake at the same time to alleviate the poverty of other peoples and of other nations. These challenges can be met only by a liberal response involving identification of the problems of change, acceptance of the need for judgment, and commitment to a program of action.

21483 J. M. HODGES LIBRARY
WHARTON COUNTY JUNIOR COLLEGE
WHARTON, TEXAS

128

DATE DUE

JAN 3 '68			
OCT 9 '68			
OCT 15 '68			
NOV 9 '72			
DEC 13 '72			
FEB 22 '73			
MAR 6 '74			
NOV 8 '74			
NOV 22 '74			
DEC 5 '74			
owed 1.00 FEB 13 '75			
JUN 20 '75			
GAYLORD			PRINTED IN U.S.A.